The One Blood

The One Blood

Kinship and Class in an Irish Village

Elliott Hastings Leyton

Newfoundland Social and Economic Studies No. 15

Institute of Social and Economic Research
Memorial University of Newfoundland

©Memorial University of Newfoundland 1975
Printed in Canada
by University of Toronto Press
ISBN 0-919666-10-8

Contents

IN MEMORY OF

My Late Father

Harry Levson, M.D.
Saskatchewan Physician and Surgeon

and

My Late Friends

Kenneth Connell, Ph.D.
Irish Historian

John Chambers
Aughnaboy Trawler Captain

Sgt. William Hall
Royal Ulster Constabulary

Preface

It is now a full decade since I first took the path which has led to this volume and to a series of articles on aspects of Northern Irish society. During the years we lived in Ulster, our spirits were particularly sustained by Mr. and Mrs. Jack Chambers, the late Sgt. and Mrs. William Hall, the late Professor K. H. Connell, Mr. and Mrs. Noel McBride, and Mr. and Mrs. Julian Crozier. To them, and to all the people of "Aughnaboy," my family and I are deeply indebted, for they did far more than simply aid our enquiry: they reshaped our psyches, enriched our lives, and taught us how to love Ulster.

The field material on which this monograph is based was collected during two extended periods of residence in Aughnaboy. The first, from September of 1964 to November of 1966, was when I was in the Department of Social Anthropology at The Queen's University of Belfast. The second, between June and December of 1969, was when I held a research appointment with Memorial University of Newfoundland's Institute of Social and Economic Research.

The volume's present form is a minor revision of a thesis submitted to the University of Toronto. I am particularly grateful to R. W. Dunning, Stuart Philpott, Sandra Wallman and Peter Carstens of the University of Toronto for their personal and intellectual support; and to my colleagues at Memorial – Robert Paine, Rex Clark, Jean Briggs, Ronald Schwartz and Frederick Johnstone – for intensive criticism. I must also record my debt to Sonia Kuryliw Paine for her invaluable editing of the manuscript, and to Jeanette Gleeson for overseeing its production.

This book is published with the assistance of a grant from the Social Science Research Council of Canada.

November, 1974
St. John's, Newfoundland   Elliott Leyton

⌐

Introduction

1

This essay has several aims. The first is narrowly ethnographic: to examine the web of kinship institutions in one European village. The study of European societies came relatively late to anthropology, but Ireland ceased to be *terra incognita* in the late 1930s with the publication of the work of Conrad Arensberg and Solon Kimball. Our understanding of the fabric of Irish social life has been further enriched by the proliferation of published material since the early 1960s.[1] Yet many lacunae remain in the Irish ethnographic record. Little is known, for example, about the north or the midlands, about urban or town society, or about religion or elite behaviour. Similarly, few attempts have been made to comprehend the diverse social forms which are contained within Ireland, for the island's cultural diversity is a phenomenon acknowledged yet unexplained. While this essay does not correct many of these omissions, it does provide ethnographic data on aspects of elite behaviour and on that cultural group about whom the least is written[2] and the least is understood – the Scots Protestants of the north. A second and more "theoretical" aim is to try to make the analysis of social class a more explicit and integral part of kinship studies. In doing so, I hope to contribute to the debate within social anthropology on the matter of the relative primacy of social structure or economics.

IRISH KINSHIP AND AUGHNABOY

The web of kinship is undoubtedly the best understood institution in Irish studies. Since the pioneering work of Arensberg and Kimball (1937, 1940), a number of anthropologists have addressed themselves to the characteristics of these fundamental social relations. If any single fact emerges from this work, it is the extraordinary variation in the significance of kinship within Ireland – and the absence of a single universal model for Irish social life or Irish kinship.

Humphreys' review of the rural Irish family, which is drawn primarily from Arensberg and Kimball's work, describes the family farm as "the centre of each individual's total activity, economic and otherwise"

---

1   Cf., for example, Arensberg and Kimball, 1968; Bax, 1970; 1971; 1973; Cresswell, 1969; Fox, 1963; 1966; 1967; 1968; Kane, 1968; Messenger, 1968; 1969; and Streib, 1973.
2   At this writing, the total corpus is Harris, 1961; 1972; and Leyton, 1966; 1970a; 1970b; 1974; 1975.

(1966:13). The strength and importance of kinship ties are reflected in the reciprocal exchange of services and in the sharing of responsibilities which characterize relations between kin. This exchange takes the form of help between kinsmen at those points in the agricultural cycle when labour requirements are at their peak – at spring ploughing, harrowing and sowing, and at summer harvest:

> But such co-operation goes on through the full round of the year and, indeed, of life. As circumstances demand it, it reciprocally binds the families of the community to provide tools, food, clothes and at times stock and even money. It requires families to supply personal services at times of childbirth, sickness, death and at important festive occasions. It governs the important matters of visiting and hospitality, and may often motivate a family to take in and raise the child of a deceased relative or friend (*ibid.*:16).

Further, these mutual obligations between kin are supported by community sanctions of estrangement and, in extreme cases, of "virtual ostracism" (*ibid.*) for failure to fulfil them.

But this pattern by no means obtains throughout Ireland. In Kane's (1968) Donegal, kinship does not appear to perform major social or economic functions, and "people are not on call to a large amorphous body of kinsmen for indiscriminate aid." While relatives may engage in minor services such as exchanging outgrown clothing, or babysitting, "such exchange is not considerably greater than among non-kin." Even on the farm, exchanges of goods and labour are conducted with non-kin as well as kin, and "when the few tools that not every farmer has are needed, or farm manure is required, a neighbor is called on more often than a relative." A similarly low functional level is reported by Cresswell (1969) in his study of the southwestern parish of Kinvarra. Here, too (p. 480), the kinship system is weak, genealogical knowledge shallow, and economic interaction between kinsmen minimal.

The source of this variation in the significance of kinship is not fully understood, but I would suggest that it lies in the nature of the resources controlled by families in a given area. Humphreys (1966) has already alluded to this matter, and indeed suggested that the strength of what he took to be the typical Irish rural family – and what distinguished the rural from the urban family – was the family's relative position in the productive process. For Humphreys, the strength of the rural family was a function of "its ownership, control, and direct operation of the principal form of productive property in the community – the farm itself" (p. 12), and this control of production gave "the farm family its own intrinsic measure of independence from non-familial organizations," and made the family farm the "centre of each individual's total activity, economic and otherwise" (p. 12 f.).

In this essay on Aughnaboy, I try to show in some empirical detail how the family's relative position with regard to the control of resources creates very different kinship patterns even within a single village. More specifically, I show how social differentiation based on the unequal distribution of wealth, prestige, and authority leads to the creation of class "groups" whose interests do not invariably coincide. In those social areas where their interests do coincide, the kinship ideology and behaviour is shared throughout the village. But in the areas where class-derived interests do not coincide, we find different interpretations of ideology and different behaviours between kinsmen. Thus, an individual's position in the class system vitally affects the ways in which he classifies his kin, conceptualizes his obligations towards them, and honours these obligations.

Ultimately, my aim is to show that kinship and class are more than simply two analytically and functionally distinct systems, one a "procreative" institution and the other a "ranking device" (Hollingshead, 1950). Rather, I try to show how kinship and class must be regarded as two interdependent systems; that the individual's position in the class hierarchy dictates and shapes many aspects of his kinship ideology; and that the kinship ideology frequently conflicts with the expectations and behaviours associated with individuals' positions in the class structure. Thus in order to comprehend the structure and function of kinship institutions in this stratified Ulster village, it is necessary to analyse not only the sets of kinship values and beliefs which all the villagers share, but also the social and economic constraints inherent in an individual's class position. It is the elicitation of this interdependence of class and kinship at the level of empirical detail which is the primary concern of this essay.

THE PRIMACY OF SYSTEMS

At the same time, it is hoped that the material contained herein will shed some light on one of the central debates in social anthropology – on the matter of which "system" is to be assigned ultimate priority in the ordering of social relations. In the ancestral tradition, Radcliffe-Brownian and Fortesian thought assigned social structure the ultimate priority. For Radcliffe-Brown (1952:198) and his followers, the wellsprings of human behaviour were to be found in the "rules of etiquette, morals and law"; and the role which other systems played was primarily as part of "the machinery for maintaining a social structure" (*ibid.*:198). Similarly, for Fortes (1949:346), it is "the basic moral axioms of a society" which regulate "the give and take of social life."

This structuralist thesis has in turn been confronted by its antithesis in the work of Peter Worsley and Edmund Leach. Here, the primacy of structure is dismissed, and replaced with the doctrine of the primacy of economics. In his extended critique of Fortes' work, Worsley (1956) returns again and again to the theme that the solidarity of structures is an

artifice, an artifice which "soon dissolves when material interests clash. ..."
"Kinship is the form which the essential relations arising from agriculture, the inheritance of property, etc., take, and as these latter relations
change, so kinship changes. Far from being basic, it is secondary"
(*ibid*.:62). For Worsley, the kinship structure "is itself the form of expression of economic and other activities," and the "significant determining
system is the economic system."

Leach reaffirms this view, arguing in *Pul Eliya* that "kinship systems
have no 'reality' at all except in relation to land and property" (1961:305);
and insisting that "the student of social structure must never forget that the
constraints of economics are prior to the constraints of morality and law"
(*ibid*.:9).

> Because the structuralists assume that the individual is constrained by *moral* forces, it
> necessarily follows that the constraint is social, and we are led directly into the Durkheimian
> mystique which attributes the characteristics of deity to Society regarded as a corporation.
> But if we repudiate the emphasis on moral rules and jural obligation then the problem becomes
> much simpler. The constraint imposed on the individual is merely one of patterning and
> limitation. ... (*ibid*.:300).

In Aughnaboy, it is the conjunction of economic and social pressures
which together create the ultimate shape of kinship institutions. Behaviour
is the "sum of many individual human actions" (Leach, 1961:300); and the
individual does indeed make his "choices so as to manipulate the system to
his advantage" (*ibid*.:133). But the individual is not operating in a moral
vacuum; and neither is he free from economic constraint. There is a
supra-statistical order in Aughnaboy, and this order is not the consequence
of random free choices: rather, it is the consequence of individuals' decisions which are informed by both the morality of kinship obligations and
the reality of economic pressure.

But I try to show how individuals' participation in a capitalist industrial
economy is the prime source of variation in the kinship "system." On the
one hand, the traditional kinship ideology provides individuals with a set of
values and beliefs associated with shared ideas about the nature of social
and biological relationships. These traditional values and expectations provide individuals with a map of the social universe and a mechanism for determining the degree of moral obligation towards their kin. But these moral
conceptions do not take place in an economic vacuum; and individuals'
participation in the industrial economy provides them with an additional
set of expectations and interests which may parallel or conflict with the
moral notions contained in the kinship structure. As an adaptation to this
potential conflict, the different social strata have developed different
ideologies regarding their moral obligations towards kin, and opposing
strategies for realizing their conflicting goals. As we shall see, it is to the
advantage of the elites to minimize extended kinship ties and maximize

non-kin contacts; and the elites' adaptation to their position in the economy is to develop a bureaucratic or "anti-kinship" model, which denies the significance of extra-familial kin. Conversely, it is to the advantage of the masses to maximize relations with kin, both familial and extra-familial, and it is here where the traditional "kinship" model of obligation and behaviour prevails.

In sum then, my argument is that in order to understand the relations between kinsmen in Aughnaboy, it is necessary for the analyst to go beyond the morality of kinship into the ambit of social stratification. For it is both the agreement of value generated by shared cultural notions and the conflict of value generated by class-derived interests and expectations, which together provide the framework for the village's kinship behaviours. But ultimately, here too, social structure "soon dissolves when material interests clash" (*op. cit.*) for morality invariably gives precedence to economics in Aughnaboy.

Part I: The Setting

Aughnaboy

2

No convenient term exists in the literature to designate the intermediate position Aughnaboy occupies between those communities described as "peasant" and those described as urban and industrial. Aughnaboy is neither of these. Yet it has characteristics of both, for what I sketch in the following pages is a synchronic picture of a society in the midst of rapid social change from a traditional peasant organization to part of an industrial economic system. The villagers are no longer peasants, "producers on a small scale, with simple equipment and market organization, often relying on what they produce for their subsistence" (Firth, 1946:22). On the contrary, the majority of the labour force is skilled and semi-skilled wage labour, and all are vitally involved in a cash economy with a relatively complex technology.

Yet neither can Aughnaboy be characterized as merely one sector of an urban industrial society, for the village is located in a highly traditional and isolated rural area. Fully half of the household heads are engaged in the ancient occupations of fishing and sailing, stone work and farming; and the villagers see themselves as distinctively rural, free from the influences of the "unfriendly" cities. With regard to these issues then, Aughnaboy – with its small farmers and company directors, its unskilled agricultural labourers and its trawler skippers – is a community whose traditional economic basis is disintegrating. Its roots lie in a peasant past, but its economic and social present is imperfectly linked to the industrialized cities of the United Kingdom. It is the consequences of this adaptation which provide the framework for the phenomena we shall examine in this volume.

HISTORICAL BACKGROUND

Aughnaboy is one village in the isolated mountainous peninsula known variously as the Glens of Perrin, the Kingdom of Perrin, and, more simply, Perrin. Perrin is an isolated but thickly populated rural area with a total population of 10,540 (1961 census), and an area of about 71 square miles, about half of which is arable. The habitation level is 600 or 700 feet above sea level at maximum, and the population is confined to a narrow strip of rolling land between the mountains and the sea.

This dense settlement between mountain and sea created a diversified ecological pattern in traditional times. According to oral history, every man in the last and preceding centuries worked as a farmer, a fisherman, and a stone man (a generic word which includes all those cutters, polishers, engravers, and masons who work with stone), according to the time of year. Nowadays individuals tend to follow one occupation, although some men fish or farm a few fields in the evenings while maintaining full-time labouring jobs.

Farming is done primarily for cash income: agriculture on the light stony soil is a mixed system, with potatoes, sheep, and oats as the primary sources – milk production being of very minor importance. The farms are small and intensively worked, fifty acres being a "good size."

Fishing, which was until recent decades "the seasonal occupation of a crofter population" (Evans, 1967:155), is now a full-time occupation for the trawlermen, and the Perrin fleet is the largest in Ireland with over forty trawlers. Evans notes that prawn fishing now occupies perhaps half of the trawler fleet throughout the year while the rest of the fleet ranges far afield; and he laments (1967:159) that "the former intimate connexions between the fishing cycle and the rhythm of life ashore have gone." Of relatively minor economic importance now, and pursued by many for sport as much as for money, is skiff fishing with lines for mackerel in the summer and trammel nets for herring in the autumn.

The stone trade has altered too. During the nineteenth century and the first third of the twentieth century, the export to Britain of dressed granite was a major source of income for the Perrins, and Perrin men boast that the streets of Liverpool are paved with their granite. By the beginning of the present century, thirty-two vessels were sailing from Aughnaboy alone to Liverpool and other English ports, carrying one hundred and fifty tons each of dressed Perrin granite (Evans, 1967:171). Since the second World War, however, the demand for granite products has declined steadily, and at the same time jobs in other industries have become available to Perrin men. While the stone trade is still an important source of income in Perrin, the family groups who worked the stone no longer occupy the dominant position they previously held in the economic life of the region.

Aughnaboy is a Protestant community which forms part of Kildarragh townland – roughly one mile wide and three miles long and stretching from the coast to the base of the Perrin Mountains. The Protestants in Perrin were not settled, as in so much of Ulster, by the Plantation of English and Scots on confiscated land. In Perrin, the Protestant population were the detached foot soldiers of the O'Neills who settled in the waste lands in the mid-sixteenth century, giving services in lieu of rent. It is to these and later

Scottish settlers "rather than to the older English planters, that Perrin owes most of its non-Irish population" (Evans, 1967:114). Today, Kildarragh townland contains both Aughnaboy and a portion of the Roman Catholic area known as Blackrock – the latter living in the mountainous third of the townland.

The village of Aughnaboy was described in the *Parliamentary Gazetter of Ireland* for 1846 as "a small village and fishing-harbour" and "the only place, along a considerable extent of bold Highland coast, where fishing vessels can find shelter."

As we pass southward through this barony of Perrin, the mountains recede a little, and the country improves in cultivation; but no kind of sea-port or creek occurs worthy of notice, excepting Aughnaboy. This little village is situated at the mouth of a considerable mountain stream, which, passing swiftly through a gully in the slate rock, serves to keep off the swell which otherwise would seem ready to bury the small craft that find shelter within. The inhabitants have cut out a little dock in the rock on the south side, which, when I saw it, was chokefull of little smacks and wherries. ... Though the village appears to be a prosperous fishing station, upwards of 250 of its inhabitants are said to have been unemployed in 1835.

Since 1851, when government census material first became available for Aughnaboy "town" – a census unit smaller than my own unit of Aughnaboy "community," which follows Aughnaboy usage – the population has followed the drift from countryside to town which is general throughout much of Ireland (see Buchanan, 1958), and Aughnaboy's population has in fact more than tripled since the Gazetter's brief visit in 1844.

The community of Aughnaboy has a population of 900 individuals distributed among 259 households. The general demographic features that distinguish the Perrin area from the rest of Northern Ireland are a high density of population, and population growth rather than stability or decline. These two characteristics, which are rarely found in rural Ireland, are possible because of the diversified and relatively prosperous economy of the area. The diversified economy of the Perrins has acted as a buffer to misfortune, and the combination of fishing, farming, and stone work as the basic sources of income made it possible for the region to adapt to changes in the national and international markets as well as to survive famine and disaster. Even during the Great Famine of the 1840s, the ready availability of fish kept the population loss through starvation and emigration to a minimum, and the Census of Ireland records only a 20 percent drop in the population of Kildarragh townland between 1841 and 1851. Thus, although relatively isolated and "traditional," Perrin has never been poor by comparison with the rest of Ireland.

Today, the economy of Aughnaboy is based on a mixture of wage labour, small businesses, stone work, and farming/fishing (see Table 1). Although the village still has the character of a fishing and sea-faring community – the houses are clustered around the harbour, a major topic of conversation is

TABLE 1

Aughnaboy's Male Household Heads, by Industry

Industry	Percentage
Fishing and Sailing	13
Stone Work	24
Farming	13
Government Employees (including permanently unemployed on welfare benefits)	10
Private Industry (non-farm/fish/stone; e.g., bakeries, petrol)	40
Total	100

the success of the fishermen, and the villagers themselves regard the community's origins and present as intimately linked with the sea – only 13 percent of the household heads are involved in full-time fishing or sailing. The majority of the population are skilled and semi-skilled wage labourers. Fifteen percent of the household heads, however, are entrepreneurs, and Aughnaboy today serves as a market town for the immediate area, with twenty-four shops – eight of them grocer's – three stone firms, an embroidery factory, an egg packaging plant, a coal distributor, and a fish processing plant.

In addition, the benefits of the Welfare State provide a large portion of many individuals' incomes, in various forms ranging from subsidies and grants for farmers and fishermen to Unemployment Insurance and National Assistance. Aughnaboy is subject to the Perrin region's high unemployment rate, which reached 20 percent in 1969. Yet few men are permanently unemployed: they lose their jobs when their construction projects are completed or when recession in seasonal demand hits their industries. But in Aughnaboy, where most men have a network of kin – or mates – to help find them jobs, where most men have skills and qualifications which are in some demand on the labour market, and where men share a belief that to be unemployed and on the dole is to reduce one's stature as a man, their unemployment tends to be a short-term problem of weeks rather than months. A man with an adequate supportive network of kin or friends is unlikely to be unemployed for more than a month in each year.

Finally, where emigration was once a necessary means of survival – by which, at the turn of the century, many of Aughnaboy's stonemen regularly spent their summers working in New York and their winters in Ireland – it is now primarily an outlet for the ambitious or the discontented. The money sent home from America and Britain is now used less for subsistence and more for the purchase of luxury goods.

BELONGING TO AUGHNABOY

If the inhabitants of Aughnaboy often work and own property outside the
village, if they have ties of kinship, affinity, and friendship which link them
to the larger society, they nevertheless form a united and self-conscious
community, whose social relations take place primarily in the village.
Those who belong to Aughnaboy grew up together; they now share a
community life and a common opposition to the enemies who surround
them. They are also linked together by beliefs in the antiquity of their
families' association: "our families have lived in Aughnaboy for hundreds
of years together"; and by the intrusion of kinship into the community
ethos: for it is believed that in the past most marriages were within the
village and those who "belong" to Aughnaboy are both neighbours and
distant kinsmen – "if you go far back enough, everybody in the village is
related." Whereas their obligations to one another are not defined in terms
of kinship, for their relationships are normally "too far out" to be
specifically recognized, the fact of their distant and ancient bonds ties them
one to another. When Tague died, the members of the non-Aughnaboy
religious sect to which he had been converted – and which prohibited all
social or ritual contact with non-members – tried to bury him; but they were
met at the church by Tague's brother and the men of Aughnaboy who
claimed their own. In the cemetery, with the men of Aughnaboy guarding
Tague's coffin from the angry members of the sect, Tague was returned to
the body of kin and community to which he belonged.

Those who belong to Aughnaboy, those whose families have lived in the
village too long for the oldest residents to remember their arrival, are
cemented together in a quasi-mystical bond of no little significance. If, in
some contexts, human beings are perceived as existing in a cold and hostile
world with only the blanket of kinship to warm them, it is also true that in
other situations, the people of Aughnaboy perceive themselves as standing
together in solidarity against the world. The village is thought of as a social
unit in a state of balance and harmony – "Aughnaboy people pull together" – whose maintenance requires that people help each other when
they can, so long as it does not sacrifice the welfare of family or kindred.
When a favourite son dies, the whole community grieves; when an emi-
grant dies abroad, his body is often returned home to be claimed by family
and community. A man will forget what he saw when his neighbour's car
moves over to the wrong side of the road and hits the tourist from Belfast.
Labour gangers will give preference to neighbours over "a complete
stranger," for not only does a relationship exist between them – "I knew
his father well" – but he is able to increase his feelings of self-esteem and to
enhance his own prestige in the village by hiring his neighbours. Labourers
seeking employment will turn to a neighbour when other bonds of support
fail: "I was out of work and desperate for it and I went to see John

Henry down the road, and he fixed me up at the scaffolding in Belfast."
When emigrating to the United States, Canada, or Australia, or simply
taking a summer's work in Scotland or England, the man of Aughnaboy will
turn first for help to his fellow-villagers who are already established in these
areas. There are construction firms in Toronto and New York, the two
most favoured cities, which employ large numbers of Aughnaboy men. If
there are no kin, affines, or friends who will receive priority, a man can
"claim" a job from an employer who also belongs to Aughnaboy. And
finally, the farmers of Aughnaboy share their labour in times of peak work
requirements such as harvesting and threshing, working each farm in turn.
If the neighbourhood tie is weaker in economic affairs than the other bonds
which unite the men of Aughnaboy, it is nevertheless real, and can be
utilized when the situation so warrants.

During social occasions, belonging to Aughnaboy means that two men
will have something to talk about, something to share. In economic situations, where one man is asking a favour of another, the fact of their shared
membership in the community means they have a greater right to a job than
a stranger. On ritual occasions, they are often *the* solidary group, for they
worship together in their own churches, they represent their village in the
religious and political festivals, and they insist upon the right to bury their
own dead.

In the political realm, the solidarity and integration of the village are
heightened by the political tension which prevails in the larger society and
by the fact that Aughnaboy is physically surrounded by hostile Catholic
communities. Protestant and Catholic houses face each other on opposite
sides of the boundary roads which divide Aughnaboy from these communities, and institutionalized social relations between them are few. It is
not, however, to be assumed from this that "Protestant" constitutes an
undifferentiated bloc; for while Protestants are united politically (against
Catholics), they differ in matters of doctrine and denomination. About
two-thirds of the village belong to the dominant high status Presbyterian
and Church of Ireland denominations, one family belongs to the Methodist
Church, and the remaining third of the village is divided among four other
denominations: Plymouth Brethren, Closed Brethren, Exclusive Brethren,
and Baptist. The latter four are low status, evangelical, and attempt to
convert or "save" members of the other denominations from the "sure
destiny of hell."

The inhabitants of Aughnaboy see their village as a collectivity in total
opposition to the Catholic enemies who surround them. They see their
village as a bastion of Protestant morality and Protestant virtue, stoutly
maintaining their faith in the face of their Catholic neighbours who are
associated not only with the freedom-denying monolith of Roman Catholicism, but also with Irish secret armies, with black magic, Communism and

Atheism. Catholics in the surrounding communities are "lying Papists," hypocritically rejecting the Crown yet living off her dole and waiting with bomb and gun to force Ulster under the rule of Dublin and Rome. The Orange Protestant Unionists see their long-term interests as intimately and irrevocably bound up with the maintenance of Northern Ireland's union with Great Britain, and their hard-won religious freedom and economic prosperity as constantly threatened by the Green Papists who wish to unite the six counties of Northern Ireland with the Republic of Ireland.

The Aughnaboy individual's view of the universe and his conception of the moral obligations between men cannot be understood until the overriding significance of Orange and Green are comprehended. Orange and Green, with their associated symbols of the Queen and Union Jack, the Pope and the Tricolour, provide the symbolic framework which structures much of Aughnaboy's political, religious, and social life. Church attendance is as much a political as a religious act, for it is a demonstration of the solidarity of the Orangemen against the Catholic foe. International politics are interpreted in these terms as well: the European Common Market, for example, is seen as part of the Catholic conspiracy to rule Europe, and the election of American President Kennedy was seen as yet another triumph for "Popery." Irish history is still vivid in the minds of the villagers; children are raised on tales of Catholic torture and betrayal of innocent Protestants, and events three centuries old are referred to as if they had occurred only recently. The corruption of the Roman Catholic Church in the Middle Ages, the Spanish Inquisition, the Protestant Heresies, the Disestablishment of the Roman Church in England, and the military victories of King William of Orange and Oliver Cromwell are seen as integral parts of present-day reality. Catholicism, with its leader the Pope, is perceived as a monolithic body of gigantic wealth and power, bent on crushing personal and religious freedom, and engaged in a ruthless campaign – which the godless English fail to understand – to dominate not only Ireland and Britain but the entire world. Protestants, on the whole, patronize Orange shops, Orange lawyers, dentists and doctors; they follow their own sports, live in their own clearly defined village and resist with force any attempt to encroach upon their territory. They send their children to "Protestant" state schools, dance to Scots music in Orange Halls, and work in Orange-dominated firms. Cross-cutting membership in any groups or associations with Catholics is minimal, and even the Women's Institute is entirely Protestant in composition.

It is perhaps not surprising that the element of laterality is used to distinguish Orange from Green. Orange and Green are "the two sides of the house," the dichotomy which characterizes the Aughnaboy individual's view of his kinsmen (matrilateral and patrilateral kin) and of his society (Orange and Green), and which influences much of his social behaviour.

One of the standard phrases – used, incidentally, by both Protestant and Catholic – for referring to "the other side" is that "they dig with the wrong (left) foot." Left is sinister, left is Green, the left side of the house conspires to control the virtuous right side; the left side tortures its victims and shoots the innocent in the back. Left is associated with the symbols of ritual and political evil – Pope and Tricolour – and right is associated with the symbols of ritual and political purity – Queen and Union Jack. It is this symbolic dichotomy between Orange and Green, with the associated political structures, which order much of the political, religious, social, and economic life.

Yet it must be understood that while Green is perceived as both the symbol and source of much Evil in Perrin, the villagers regard the surrounding Catholics as equally and fully human, only misguided and perverted by heretical doctrines and evil institutions. This recognition of the essential humanity of the other side – "we're all the one blood if you go back far enough" – is reflected even in times of extreme political tension, when the violence which occurs in Perrin is directed primarily towards objects rather than things. This notion of a shared humanity is derived partly from their shared consciousness as "men of Perrin." Protestant and Catholic share not only the common dialect (the distinctive Perrin blend of Scots and Irish) which distinguishes them from all other English speakers, but also a strong sense of moral and physical superiority to all other men. Morally, they are superior to the English, the Protestants despising them for their "snobbery," their "moral decadence," their political naivety and their "unfriendliness," while the Catholics despise them for their "ruthless" oppression of the Irish.

Perhaps more important than this sense of regional identity is their recognition of a culture, of a set of values shared by both Protestants and Catholics which distinguishes them from all outsiders – a phenomenon I have described in some detail elsewhere (Leyton, 1974). Regarding appropriate behaviour towards "strangers" (all non-kin), they are all expected to behave according to the model of cheerfulness and friendliness which I have described elsewhere under the folk concept of "decency" (Leyton, 1966). Similar expectations and moral obligations are also associated with the kinship system, both Orange and Green having strikingly similar postulates about kin classification and behaviour. They share a set of common values and priorities on the basis of which they construct their prestige hierarchies. And finally, they share a common ideology regarding the workings of the political system, for both conceive of it as a patronage system, distributing its largesse to the supporters of the men in power (what is in dispute is merely who should have the power).

However, the impression should not be given that the people of Aughnaboy live in complete harmony with their Catholic neighbours. Riots and bombings of buildings and monuments have occurred in times of political tension. Further, in our study of the moral obligations which bind human beings to one another, the Orange/Green dichotomy is the one principle which relieves a Protestant from Aughnaboy of the obligation to aid or assist someone on "the other side." The moral obligations and structural constraints which occupy the remainder of this essay exist only between Protestants, for Protestants marry only Protestants, and the conventions of kinship cannot structure the behaviour between Orange and Green.

Social Class in Aughnaboy

3

The ultimate concern of this monograph is kinship; but it is necessary to examine social class in some detail because the stratification system has such a profound impact on kinship ideology and behaviour in Aughnaboy. This follows logically from several basic sociological propositions. Individuals are assigned sets of "patterned expectations defining the *proper* behaviour of persons playing certain roles" by the stratification system (Parsons, 1954:61). Different roles involve different expectations and potentially conflicting interests. These structurally generated role interests are what Dahrendorf has described as "undercurrents of his behaviour which are predetermined for him for the duration of his incumbency of a role" (1959:179).

The occupants of similar positions or roles "find themselves in a common situation" (*ibid*.:179), as when two trawler skippers are expected to maximize their catches and the efficiency of their crews. Occupants of different positions, say of domination and subjection, hold "certain interests which are contradictory in substance and direction" (*ibid*.:174), as when a stone yard owner is committed to the efficiency of his employees and his enterprise, while his employees are often expected to use their influence on behalf of their kinsmen. While those who share a similar class position can be thought of as sharing certain vital interests and behaving in similar ways – as distinct from and in opposition to those in dissimilar positions – they cannot be regarded as constituting a "group." "Just as all doctors ... do not as such constitute social groups, the occupants of positions with identical ... interests are not a group," for "groups are masses of people in regular contact or communication, and possessing a recognizable structure" (*ibid*.:180). Throughout this study then, I shall refer to those who share a similar position in the class hierarchy as an "aggregate," or a "stratum."

My argument is a simple one. The men of Aughnaboy have important links which bind them to their families and wider kindred. In conceptualizing their responsibilities towards these kin, they share a wide range of values, beliefs, and behaviours which I shall refer to as kinship *consensus*. For most men, the significance of this consensus is bolstered by the peculiar economic climate in which jobs are well-paid but short-term, and it becomes highly convenient to use kin as a regular form of insurance policy for jobs and other financial aid. Thus in this sense, the continuing reciprocal exchange of valued services takes place against a backdrop of a consensus ideology which extends rights and duties to a wide range of kin.

At the same time, however, the differential distribution of prestige, authority, and wealth creates distinct and separate class strata in Aughnaboy; and membership in different strata carries with it expectations and interests which are often in conflict with the interests of individuals in other strata. It is at this point in the structure, where the differing interests of the various class strata collide, that what I call *dissensus* in kinship ideology and behaviours becomes apparent; and it is here that social class phenomena generate differentiation in the actual behaviour between kin. In sum then, my argument is that in order to understand Augnaboy's kinship system, it is necessary to understand not only the agreement of value (consensus) in kinship ideology and behaviour which arises out of basic notions in the culture about kinsmen, but also the disagreement of value (dissensus) which stems from the unequal distribution of prestige, authority, and wealth; that is, the conflicting interests of the elites and the masses.

THE STRATIFICATION SYSTEM

Social class and kinship are major, if not *the* major fields of empirical enquiry in the social sciences. Anthropologists have by no means been unaware of the significance of social class; Pitt-Rivers (1960), for example, has observed that "the concept of social class is central to the discussion of the structure of any modern European community." In the light of this, it is curious how little explanatory role has been assigned to social class in European anthropological studies. Doubly curious is the scanty attention which has been paid to the empirical linkage of class and kinship.

Firth *et al.* (1969) have attempted to link the two, remarking that "it might be held that in modern times kinship is most marked at either end of the social scale, corresponding to social needs of very different kinds" (*ibid.*:14). The general pattern they observed in their London study was one in which kin ties "seem to be still important in the transmission of economic and political assets" among the upper classes. On the other hand, among the working classes, where these assets are rare, "the strength of kin ties is to be correlated with their relatively weak and unprotected social and economic position" (*ibid.*:15). Finally, the "kinship attitudes of the middle classes [are] somewhere between the interest in perpetuation of economic and political assets shown by the upper classes and the warm protectiveness of the propertyless working classes" (*ibid.*:16).

On the whole, however, class and kinship have been regarded as separate fields of enquiry and sometimes as quite separate social systems, with a structure and function that are "essentially different" (Hollingshead, 1950); where "the family is the procreative and primary training institution, whereas the class system functions as a ranking device."

An additional problem in anthropological class analysis has been that of establishing "a single system of stratification by asking the inhabitants to rank their neighbours in terms of class or prestige" (Pitt-Rivers, 1960). Arensberg and Kimball, for example, constructed their system of stratification by "grouping together those that have common features in the eyes of the people of the town" (1968:324). Using the dimension of prestige, they grouped their townsmen into seven social categories which they regarded as the community's class structure.

The people of Ennis know their "places." They are for the most part keenly aware of social standing, position, and class. As in any community, "appearances" must be kept up. Class does not make for aloofness as it does in metropolitan regions, for everyone lives more or less in sight of everyone else. Nor do the folkways demand as in America that a pretense of social democracy be kept up. Each man knows fairly well what to expect of the other and respects the difference. Superiority and inferiority are relative matters. There are infinite gradations. But there are broad outlines none the less, and a man knows the "station" that is his. ... There are always those who, others will tell you, have "come down in the world." But everybody is agreed on the directions, on "up" and on "down" (*ibid*.:322–23).

In the analysis of kinship in Aughnaboy which follows, I focus on three dimensions of social class:[1] prestige, wealth, and authority. For the relationship between class and kinship is a complex and multi-dimensional matter, in which prestige strata may affect marriage, wealth strata may affect inheritance, and authority strata may influence attitudes towards hiring kin.

I shall concentrate on teasing out the varying impact of these three dimensions upon the kinship system. Membership in the different aggregates or strata is not identical, for "it is, perhaps, self-evident that inequalities of class, status and power need not always coincide" (Runcimann, 1969). The varying distribution of these commodities can place two individuals who occupy the same stratum in one dimension (say, prestige) in two different strata along another dimension (say, wealth). Thus, a labour ganger and a stone yard owner both belong to the same authority stratum, for both hire and fire workers, and both will have similar interests regarding the employment of kinsmen. Yet the two belong to different strata in the prestige dimension, and will act differently regarding, say, a proposed marriage between their children. This differing membership in the three dimensions of social class is summarized in Table 2.

But whereas there is some ambiguity in the assignation of different dimensions and in the precise boundaries which can be drawn, it should be clear that all three of these dimensions are ultimately linked to a *single*

1   Throughout the remainder of this monograph, I use "social class" as a general term for referring to the three dimensions of inequality – prestige, power, and wealth. In doing so, I follow Dahrendorf who writes that social class indicates "an area and a type of sociological analysis rather than its substance," and that the term is therefore more useful in general compounds such as "class structure" (1959:204–05).

TABLE 2

Strata Formed by the Three Dimensions of Social Class in Aughnaboy

Dimension	Percentage of Male Household Heads	Broad Proportions
Prestige		
First: Directors or owners of large firms, higher professionals, and independently wealthy.	3	"Upper class" = 6%
Second: Professionals	3	
Third: Trawler owners, larger farmers, medium-size business owners.	5	"Middle class" = 26%
Fourth: Small businessmen, medium-size farmers, salesmen and clerical workers.	14	
Fifth: Skippers, foremen, labour gangers, and contractors.	7	
Sixth: Skilled labourers and semi-skilled (including fishermen).	46	"Working class" = 68%
Seventh: Unskilled labourers, sailors.	22	
Authority		
First: Those who both own and control their enterprises and hiring; e.g., stone yard owner.	15	Upper = 21%
Second: Those who control hiring, but do not own the enterprise; e.g. foreman.	6	
Third: Neither ownership nor control, but a degree of influence; e.g. stone yard artisan.	68	Lower = 79%
Fourth: Those without influence, ownership, or control; e.g., chronically unemployed labourer.	11	
Wealth		
First: Those who own major items of capital large enough to provide primary source of income; e.g., trawler, farm, stone yard.	25	Upper = 25%
Second: Those who do not own such capital.	75	Lower = 75%

phenomenon: the relation of individuals to the means of production in a capitalist industrial economy. Ultimately, individuals' access to all three scarce social commodities (prestige, authority over hiring, and wealth) is a function of their position in the economic hierarchy. As such, in the concluding chapter, I return to a unidimensional analytic scheme which tries to explain differential behaviour in terms of a simpler stratification model of 'elites' and 'masses.'

PRESTIGE STRATA

Farber (1971:8) has observed that "the most valuable property of a kin group aside from wealth is its position among other kinship units in terms of honour and status." In Aughnaboy, the community allocates different levels of honour or prestige to individuals, the degree of which is the village's statement of his worth. It is not just an individual who is ranked however, for an individual's rank influences and is, in turn, influenced by the rank of his family and close kin, especially those who bear the same surname. The rise in prestige of a man's patrinominal kin will bear on his own prestige and, conversely, the fall of his kin will reflect upon him. This close linkage of individual with kin in the eyes of the community strengthens the mutual dependence of kinsmen; indeed, it adds another brick to the wall which isolates them from the world of non-kin. In general, individuals are enjoined to do more than simply maintain the *status quo*, to do more than "competing to remain equal" (Bailey, 1971:19). In Aughnaboy, a man's responsibility is to conserve his own prestige; but his goal is to maximize his own and his family's reputation. Thus, prestige is continually being redistributed over the generations. Economic conditions change and so too do the performances of families, and, over time, individuals and families rise and fall in the public esteem accorded them.

The prestige strata in which the inhabitants of Aughnaboy are ranked are not perfectly and objectively distinguishable "groups," for boundaries are blurred, and it is proper to speak of a continuum. Within this continuum however, levels of prestige can be distinguished enough to permit the analyst to say that some individuals are ranked closely together into what could be called strata. Three broad prestige strata (see Table 2) are formed on the basis of the "differences in social attributes and styles of life which are accorded higher or lower prestige" (Dunning, 1960). An individual is placed in his prestige stratum on the basis of his occupation: once placed within his stratum, the additional factors of his "blood," his "decency," and his spirituality modify his position within that stratum.

Occupation

Occupation is the primary criterion used by the community in assessing an individual's public performance, and it is this single variable which ultimately places him in his prestige stratum. The remaining characteristics can only move him up or down within the single stratum. Occupation is what gives a man his character and his worth; for Aughnaboy is Protestant and Puritan in the Weberian mould. High praise is reserved for the man who, while avoiding any elaborate displays of consumption, works from dawn to dusk in a lifelong struggle to maximize his resources; hard work is considered good and success better, and only "worthless layabouts" would, it is felt, denigrate these values or fail to act according to them. With these values then, men select their occupations on the basis of the maximum prestige they can derive from them; for they know that their choice will fix their place in society for their lifetime.

Occupations are ranked relative to one another in seven categories (see Table 2), according to the attributes of the work which are valued by the community; these attributes are the income the job provides, the existence of manual labour, the amount of education necessary for the job, and the power over their fellows which individuals derive from their position. Thus, in the highest occupational rank would be owners of large businesses, higher professionals, and those of independent means; in the lowest categories are the unskilled labourers who do heavy manual labour for low wages and exercise little influence in the affairs of their fellows.

But a man's total prestige is not simply a function of his occupation, and the ranking of the secondary characteristics of blood, "decency," and spirituality can alter his relative position within his occupational stratum; thus, a sexually promiscuous doctor or a lawyer with "bad blood" would rank at the bottom of the 'higher professional' stratum, while a devoted son and religious stone mason would rank at the top of his stratum.

Blood

A man's "blood," the physical and moral qualities of his ancestors, gives him the prestige he will bear as a child; upon his reaching adulthood, this blood modifies the prestige accorded him by the community on the basis of his occupation. Thus, blood, like a man's "decency" or his spirituality, is capable of pushing him up or down within his stratum. The significance of *the one blood* is a consequence of the villagers' beliefs that biological reproduction transmits not only physical characteristics, but also personality and worth. It follows from this then that a man *is* his ancestors: besides sharing their name and their estate, he takes on also their psychic and social qualities. If a man's kin are dour and phlegmatic, then it is expected he will be as well. In this way too honour is transmitted; however, "the blood is strongest" in the male line, and a man's prestige normally follows that of his father's people. The prestige of his mother's family is of significance only if it is extremely high or low; thus if his mother's family's prestige is very low because of their poverty, their quarrelsomeness, their promiscuity, or their work at menial occupations, then it will mitigate or even overrule his father's prestige. Normally, marriages between unequals do not occur, and a man inherits the prestige of his father and grandfather on the basis of these beliefs about the nature of reproduction.

Decency

The variable of "decency" is essentially a communal assessment of an individual's interactional style. A decent man is one who behaves with his kin and his neighbours according to norms which insist upon the public display of friendliness, cheerfulness, and calm. Thus an individual must always be ready to stop and chat, to "pass the time of day," in an egalitarian and open manner. More importantly, under no circumstances must he allow himself to display fear, insecurity, or aggression, for it is these emotions which will lower the public repute of a man. The highest praise in Aughnaboy is reserved for the individuals who maintain an aura of jovial friendliness under any provocation: "he's the decentest, civilest man I know; nothing you say can make him angry." In addition, he must temper friendliness with sobriety and self-deprecation, minimizing the significance of his successes, deprecating as "only natural" the strength of his devotion to his kin, and calling public attention to his failures. The more closely an individual approximates these values, the higher the level he will achieve within a single prestige stratum; and the less he displays these characteristics, the more he will plummet to the bottom of his occupational stratum.

Spirituality
The significance of this characteristic is apparent in two principal areas; a man's separation from his "animal nature" (that is, his sexuality) and his religious devotion. Men are seen as locked in a constant struggle between their spirituality and the base forces of sexuality; and those who publicly allow their sexuality to conquer them must suffer. Similarly, a man must control the sexuality of his close female kin (his wife, daughters, sisters) and he must ensure that marital sex is a calm affair of moderate frequency and absolute fidelity. For a sister to "have to get married," for a man to "bother" his wife so much that she is pregnant again within a few months of the birth of her previous child – these are acts which denigrate the spirituality of a man and lower individuals in the eyes of the community, for they are seen as a capitulation to the animal and base nature of man and a rejection of the spiritual message of Christianity.

Another element in the assessment of one's spirituality is membership and participation in a particular religious denomination. The seven Protestant denominations with churches in Aughnaboy are ranked into two prestige strata, the established churches whose total membership makes up two-thirds of the population of Aughnaboy; and the evangelical denominations which comprise the remaining third of Aughnaboy. To preserve their prestige, individuals must remain loyal to their inherited membership in the high-prestige denominations: they must ignore the siren call of the evangelists' revival tent meetings. A woman must resist the impulse to marry a man of a lower denomination (women assume their husbands' denominations at marriage), for to do so would compromise the position of her children. To ensure the purity and loyalty of their congregations, the villagers discourage social interaction between the strata; members of the established denominations do so because they say the evangelicals are inferior in spirituality and worth; and members of the evangelical denominations say the established denominations are spiritually misguided, stained by "Romish" (that is, Catholic) ritual, and "bent for the Fires of Hell and Damnation." Finally in this regard, a man must be seen participating in the affairs of his denomination, sending his wife and children to church on Sundays and making occasional appearances himself, as well as contributing to the church and publicly affirming his faith in doctrine and ritual. To do otherwise is to risk the accusation of godlessness.

In sum then, families share a level of prestige assigned them by the community, and this prestige influences and is influenced by the prestige accorded a man's wider kin. Occupation fixes a man at a single level of prestige, and "blood," "decency," and spirituality determine an individual's place within that occupational level. Thus a doctor, who belongs to the first stratum on the basis of his occupation, will be ranked within that stratum on the basis of modifying characterisitcs; so it is that Horace Brady, the doctor who owns and operates the stone yard his grandfather created, and whose behaviour and spirituality are unimpeachable, occupies the highest position in his stratum and the highest position in the village. Edwards, the chronically unemployed, unskilled labourer, whose sexual affairs are the scandal of the village, and whose interactional style is "cold" and reserved, occupies the bottom rung in his stratum and in his village.

AUTHORITY STRATA

An additional dimension of social class which profoundly influences kinship relations is authority; specifically, over hiring and firing. By authority, I follow conventional sociological usage in referring to that legitimate power which is vested in social positions and roles, to what Dahrendorf (1959:166) calls "the legitimate relation of domination and subjection."

Authority over jobs, over hiring and firing, is particularly vital in Aughnaboy because, even though it is a prosperous part of Ireland, jobs there are of fragile tenure. More than 60 percent of the men are employed as wage-labourers, generally in road building or on construction sites – industries whose jobs are short-term and insecure – and are constantly subject to lay-offs from seasonal and long-term variations in the industries. Bott (1971:254) has already observed that such conditions of "acute job uncertainty" can have profound effects on kinship ties. In Aughnaboy, kinship bonds become major channels for sharing information about new jobs and arranging the hiring of kin. An individual's kindred act as a form of job insurance, providing him with the information and influence required to keep his present job, or to obtain a new and better-paying one.

Authority over hiring and firing is only a minute portion of the spectrum of power in Aughnaboy, but it is in this area that power and authority intrude in major ways upon the kinship system. Unlike prestige which is diffused among the family and the kindred, authority is vested in the individual alone. Empirically, the different occupations can be classified into four strata on the basis of their relative degree of authority over hiring accorded their occupational roles. The first two strata (see Table 2) comprising the elite represent 21 percent of the male household heads in Aughnaboy including stone yard owners, skippers and foremen – those who own and/or control their enterprises, and whose obligations include the supervision of recruitment. In the following chapters, I shall try to show how membership in the elite strata invests the individuals with expectations and interests which alter their perceptions of their obligations towards kin and their consequent behaviour. The lower strata, the Masses, have no formal authority in the hiring process, but can be observed empirically to exercise varying degrees of influence. Here I refer to the 68 percent of the male household heads who can, in fact, use influence in pressing for the hiring of a kinsman or in alerting a kinsman of a forthcoming vacancy in his yard or on his trawler.

Accession to the authority roles in the elite strata is not, at our level of enquiry, a complex matter. Individuals enter the elite either through the inheritance of enterprises or by "working their way up" in an organization, gaining the confidence of the owner to the point where he is granted a skipper's berth or a foreman's position; or, by creating his own enterprise – buying a trawler for example, or setting himself up as a labour ganger, organizing labour teams for Belfast's construction sites.

The role the individual comes to occupy carries with it sets of expectations; generally, members of the authority elite have interests requiring them to subordinate all obligations to the viability of their enterprise, whereas the masses' interests are to divide their loyalties between their enterprise and their kinsmen.

WEALTH STRATA

A third and final dimension of social class in Aughnaboy remains to be discussed. I refer to the considerable differences in wealth which distinguish the villagers. The precise amount of wealth owned in Aughnaboy is impossible to elicit from informants, given the secrecy which surrounds these affairs. It can, however, be asserted that the personal wealth held by individuals ranges from £100 or less in goods and cash held by, for example, a chronically unemployed labourer, to a stone yard and house owned by a village entrepreneur which should be valued in excess of £50,000. Judging from the amounts of wealth circulating at inheritances (see Ch. 7), the more "typical" level of personal wealth ranges from £500 to £2,000.

However, a grading of class strata based on the distribution of wealth is not germane to our purpose here; rather, what is crucial is a crude dichotomy based on the ownership of major items of capital. By this I mean those assets which enable an individual to derive all or most of his income from them and which provide an income sufficient to render outside employment unnecessary. Here I wish to distinguish between that 25 percent of Aughnaboy's population who are owners of capital such as farms, shops, trawlers, and blocks of cash large enough to provide an investment income, and the remaining 75 percent who do not own such capital. Although these capital items range in value from a small confectionery shop worth perhaps £1,500 to a stone yard worth £50,000, they are similar in that their owners derive the bulk of their income from them.

The possession of these assets creates a class stratum with interests and expectations which are different from and, occasionally, conflict with the interests of the stratum which does not control such assets. It is perhaps to be expected that the zone of dissensus here is primarily in the area of inheritance and, indeed, in chapter 7, I shall try to show how the ownership of these major items of capital creates considerable dissensus in an otherwise shared and consensual inheritance ideology.

In sum, I have described the dimensions of class which influence the village's kinship ideology and behaviour. Two broad class groups, the elites and the masses, coalesce around the dimensions of inequality, and all are ultimately related to individuals' differential positions in the economic hierarchy. The chapters which follow examine these matters in some detail, and attempt to give ethnographic flesh to the theoretical problems discussed above.

Part II: Institutions

The Family

4

The family is the social unit of paramount importance for all class strata in Aughnaboy. It is especially important here because there are no large-scale corporate kin groups, and from no other social unit can men claim and expect to receive total loyalty. Yet while this attitude is shared throughout the village, the conflicting interests of the different class strata introduce dissensus and conflict into the important areas of adoption, residence, and the relations between fathers and sons.

THE HOUSEHOLD

For all class strata, the household is a residential unit which normally consists of a married couple and their unmarried children. The patrilocal extended family household characteristic of Arensberg and Kimball's (1940) County Clare is a rarity in Aughnaboy, where the predominance of the elementary family household is primarily a function of the high value placed on independent households for married couples and of the fact that cheap rented housing is relatively easy to obtain. The 900 inhabitants of Aughnaboy are distributed among approximately 259 households.

The members of a household are recruited through kinship and affinity (by affinity, I refer exclusively to spouses: a woman, for example, would never bring her brother to live with her in her husband's house); 69 percent of all households contained only parents and unmarried children, and only 7 percent contained representatives of more than two generations. Only kinsmen and spouses feel comfortable living in the same dwelling; only three households contained persons who were not kin or spouses of household members: Johnny Hazard's mistress/shop assistant lived with him, a kinless invalid pensioner lived with her nurse, and Henry Tague took in a neighbour's illegitimate daughter whose stepfather had "thrown her out of the house." Members of the various households occupy one of the house types which predominate in the area: Victorian stone dwellings of one or two storeys, semi-detached houses characteristic of the housing estates, or modern detached bungalows.

While each household is linked through the ties of kinship and affinity with other households within and outside Aughnaboy, each household is also in a sense an autonomous unit. The household is the fundamental unit of solidarity in all social strata in Aughnaboy. Its members share in common the prestige assigned them by the rest of the community and to offend one member of a household is to offend them all. It is virtually impossible to persuade one member of a household to comment adversely, however mildly, upon another. It is only within the household (and family) that it is possible for emotions to be freely displayed, and for the secrecy which often surrounds relations with outsiders to be dropped. It is only here that an atmosphere of absolute trust and loyalty can inform social relations. Further, although the ownership of property is normally vested in individuals and the household as a group rarely owns property in common, each household is nevertheless an economic entity. Income tax and rates or rents are usually paid for the household as a whole. Income and expenditure are usually shared in that the income of the father and a substantial portion of the income of any working children are pooled and used for joint expenditure in the normal day-to-day running of the house, in the purchase of luxury goods, and in saving. Finally, it is the household which is the unit of representation in community affairs. Only one donation to church or charity is expected from each household, regardless of the number of working members it may contain; and only one representative from each household is expected to attend the funeral or wake of a non-kinsman.

The Aughnaboy household has two dominant characteristics: it is numerically small and genealogically simple. As I have said above, a household is normally made up of a married couple and their unmarried children, and in fact, the average household size is but 3.5 persons. Further, only 18 of the 259 households contain more than two generations. This simplicity is not, however, a function of economic need: the domestic unit is not small and autonomous as it is, for example, among Stenning's (1962) pastoral Fulani, because natural conditions including seasonal variations and natural hazards dictate a high degree of "autonomy in the smallest social units." On the contrary, the household is small and autonomous in Aughnaboy because the villagers believe that having more than two generations in one house would lead to serious quarrels over autonomy – "you can't have two women running the same house," and because of the marked sense of impropriety which is associated with the idea of children engaging in sexual activity in a parent's household. The consequent practice is that at marriage, and especially at the birth of the first child, a couple normally sets up an independent residence.

More important is the phenomenon of adoption; for it is here that dissensus in values and behaviour becomes apparent between the strata. While all the villagers believe that to adopt non-kin is a dangerous act, and is courting catastrophe by bringing "strange" and potentially dangerous blood into the household, beliefs diverge among the wealth strata on the issue of adopting kin. Those who are not owners of major items of capital

TABLE 3

Household Composition in Aughnaboy

Household Type	Age of Household Head				
	20–29	30–49	50–64	65–	Totals
Elementary *(parent(s) and unmarried children)*	18	75	48	38	179
Extended *(parent(s) and at least 1 married child)*	0	4	3	10	17
Joint *(2 siblings or more, at least 1 of whom is married)*	0	2	4	4	10
Sibling *(at least 2 siblings, all single)*	0	0	2	3	5
Solo *(widowed or divorced)*	0	0	7	16	23
Solo *(unmarried)*	0	1	5	8	14
Affinal	0	0	0	2	2
Kindred	0	2	4	0	6
Non-kin	0	0	0	3	3
Total	18	84	73	84	259

believe that it would be "cruel and inhuman" to adopt a kinsman; to take a child from its mother and the warmth of the family hearth is to risk serious damage to his psyche. Indeed, they are often horrified at the suggestion of such adoptions, and even deny that they exist in Aughnaboy.

However, owners of major items of capital tend to de-emphasize such fears for the psychological development of the child. Although they express their concern about the adopted child's feeling "jealous" of the siblings he left behind, they emphasize the important economic and social benefits which can be bestowed upon the child, as well as "the joy of having two mothers," which the child receives in return for his "sacrifice." Those who do not have children of their own are placed in a difficult position, for they are enjoined to transmit their property to close kin, and preferably to children; they can rectify this situation by "adopting" a sibling's child. An exchange occurs here in which the property owner offers his legacy to, say, his nephew, in return for the "comfort" of the child's company in his declining years.

The normal arrangement is for the childless property owner to ask a sibling, generally a poorer one, for a child. If his request is honoured, he takes the child into his home – generally at the age of eight to eleven, for it is believed that to do so earlier or later would make the adjustment too difficult for the child – and raises the child as his own. When the owner dies, his property passes to the adopted child in fulfillment of the informal contract. It was under these conditions that Fitch, an aging bachelor with a "fine farm of land," took his labourer brother's son into his own household and willed the farm to the child. Similarly, Miss M'Cree, the heiress to a large cash inheritance, "adopted" her sister's two daughters; the girls left their labourer father's home and their four siblings and moved across the road to their aunt's house and their future estate.

This institution of adoption, however, is not always a happy affair for the beneficiaries. After repeated urgings, the mother of an impoverished family capitulated and allowed her fifth son to be adopted by her sister, stating publicly that William and his aunt were inseparable "friends" and referring obliquely to the "fine prospects" of the grocery shop and house which awaited her son. The move occurred, and William was raised in his aunt's home from the beginning of his twelfth year. Now, in middle age, William often remarks on his bewilderment at the time of the adoption, his not knowing whether to be pleased that his aunt loved him so much or to be hurt that his mother loved him so little. Frequently, he chose the latter response, and even now can neither "forgive" his mother for her decision nor suppress his jealousy of his brothers who shared their mother's home throughout their childhood.

Yet, in spite of the bitterness such decisions make, the institution of intra-familial adoption endures in Aughnaboy, for it presents a solution to many social dilemmas: the selection of a recipient for an estate, the loneliness of the old and childless, and the desire for social mobility. Similarly, the institution endures in spite of the ideological dissensus I have described.

For most of the villagers, however, household composition is not a complex matter. The composition of any one household is not fixed, but rather continually passes through the phases of the development cycle. The changes closely follow the three phases in the cycle delineated by Fortes (1962). The first phase of expansion begins with the marriage of two people and lasts "until the completion of their family of procreation." During this phase, children live with their parents and are subject to their discipline and instructions. This phase normally begins for a man in his late twenties or early thirties and continues until his late fifties when his own children begin to marry and his family of procreation enters the phase of dispersion, which continues until all the children are married. In Aughnaboy, where one daughter often remains unmarried and stays at home to care for her aging parents, this phase never ends for some of the villagers. Yet most of the population do marry, and proceed to the third and final phase of their family's developmental cycle in their sixties, the phase of replacement, which ends "with the death of the parents and the replacement in the social structure of the family they founded by the families of their children" (op. cit.).

RESIDENCE

Slightly more than two thirds (73 percent of sampled marriages) of the villagers marry people from outside the community. This pattern is not, however, a function of any exogamous proscriptions forbidding marriage within the village. Rather, it is primarily a consequence of the belief that "if you go back far enough" (in their genealogies), all the villagers would be found to be related. Thus, they reason, marriage between two villagers runs the risk of marriage between close kin; that is, deformed and enfeebled children. The result is that in most Aughnaboy marriages, one of the couple's natal families lives in another village, and a decision must be made about which natal family to live near.

There is one important notion regarding residence which is shared by all the villagers, and that is that there should be only one "woman of the house." For if there are two, even if it is mother and daughter, quarrels would be inevitable over running the house and caring for the children, and embarrassment would be felt about two sexually active couples living in the same household. The solution to these problems is a strong preference in all class strata for new and independent households for married couples; and unless poverty makes such a step impossible, each new couple normally sets up an independent household. With the exception of the first few months of marriage when the young wife's fear of leaving home – or of pregnancy – often prevents the immediate establishment of a new household, the ideal is closely adhered to in Aughnaboy.

Here, as with adoption, residential practices follow class lines. The two strata, delineated on the basis of ownership of major capital, have very different ideologies. Those who own capital operate according to a rigid patrilocality similar to that described by Arensberg and Kimball (1940) for County Clare. In this stratum, the inheritance of, say, a stone yard, carries with it a responsibility to ensure that the reputation and importance of "the name" is maintained in the village. Additionally, a house – "the home place" – is normally associated with major capital, and a family house will normally be inherited along with a stone yard or farm. Thus, for both social and practical reasons, it is desirable for men who inherit these capital items to bring their wives with them to Aughnaboy; to insist that "it is only right" that, at marriage, women come to their husbands' village. In this manner, the news agent Meadows, who owned his own shop in Aughnaboy, continued to live there when he married a girl from a poor and low-prestige Drumkil family. Similarly, Taylor, a second generation bread-server, who married an Aughnaboy girl whose family owned houses and a shop, came to Aughnaboy.

Among those who do not own major items of capital, however, there is a different ideology, one which extends preferences for propinquity equally to both male and female. Here the notion is that both husband and wife are entitled to live near their natal kin, and everyone should try to do so.

Among those whose decision is not dictated by the possession of major capital, the additional dimension of prestige becomes significant, and hence, moving away from one's kin at marriage is virtually an admission of their social inferiority. Moving away suggests 1) that their worth (kin) is so limited that their wishes can be overlooked; 2) that kin are so lacking in influence and wealth as to be unable to arrange housing for their newly married kin; 3) that quarrels may have divided the family. Furthermore, a man's moving to his wife's village is often seen as an admission that his personality and character are weaker than his wife's – for otherwise he would have prevailed upon her to move to his village.

Leaving one's natal village is forcing oneself to live among "strangers," to condemn oneself to a life of loneliness away from the focus of one's affection and the source of one's strength. With the passing of time these considerations become less acute: the woman raises her own family which becomes the focus of her emotional life, and meanwhile, she makes frequent visits by bus and by car to the home of her mother and sisters. The man makes friends with other kinless individuals, and gradually feels less like a stranger in his adopted village. Yet at the time of the marriage these are unknown qualities, and years filled with loneliness seem to stretch before the stranger, since only one spouse can normally be satisfied by the residence preferences.

Unless practical considerations intervene (the wife's parents may live too far away from his work), the matter is resolved by the couple's assessment of the relative prestige of the two families. A couple then normally chooses to live in the village of the higher ranking family, for to do so would reflect favourably upon themselves and their children, as well as increase the likelihood of the dispensation of material favours. In practice, these considerations are resolved as often in favour of the bride's village as of the groom's (of the twenty-eight sampled marriages with one spouse recruited from outside Aughnaboy, fourteen live in the husband's village and fourteen in the wife's). Thus McDonagh, a young apprentice plumber from a poor Drumkil family, willingly moved to Aughnaboy when he married the daughter of McLandress, a wealthy Aughnaboy fisherman; and Agnew, from Ballykeel, rented a house next to the five adjacent Aughnaboy homes where his wife's mother and married sisters live.

Nevertheless, the potential conflict inherent in this situation is considerable, for any decision must assault the esteem of the "losing" family. To ameliorate this, a *public fiction* is maintained that there is a critical housing shortage in Perrin, a problem which made it impossible for the couple to find a house in the losing family's village. Thus, the lower prestige family, whose honour has been slighted by the young couple, can explain the decision in terms of the critical housing shortage; indeed, the villagers continually complain about the impossibility of finding housing, in spite of the fact that it is readily available. On the other hand, the "winning" family will privately explain the couple's decision in terms of the profound and "natural" desire of their child to continue to live near its parents, while carefully couching any discussions of the subject with the "losing" parents in terms of the impossibility of finding housing. An illustration of this process is provided by the case of Alice, the daughter of a successful Aughnaboy contractor, who announced her engagement to Geordie, the son of a socially superior Ballykeel chemist. The announcement triggered a struggle which continued up to a week before the marriage. Privately, the couple had already made their decision before the engagement was announced: they would live in Ballykeel; and their public explanation of this was the conventional one, to wit, that no housing was available in Aughnaboy. This would normally have terminated the dilemma, but Alice's parents were persistent and anxious to avoid the slight of having their daughter move away. Consequently, they offered the young couple a cottage which the family owned in the centre of Aughnaboy, depriving Alice of her plea that no houses were available. This forced Geordie to counter that his residence was necessary in Ballykeel, because Aughnaboy was seven miles away and commuting to work would have been an inconvenient and impossible task. Before Alice's parents could offer to buy Geordie a car, Geordie's parents suggested that Alice merely move into Geordie's room in the family house and that "they can look for a house next year."

If even such manipulations fail to give a measure of satisfaction to both parties and the couple can choose neither village without irrevocably offending one family, the common path then is for them to claim that "there isn't a decent house" in either village, and to settle in a third, It should be clear, however, that the absence of a unilateral residence rule and the presence of different class strata with different interests and expectations together generate dissensus and conflict.

FAMILY ROLES

A man of Aughnaboy, like men of other societies, belongs to two families in the course of his life. Before marriage, his loyalty lies with his family of origin; after marriage and the birth of his children, his loyalties must expand to include his own family of procreation. The four sets of familial roles are central to the universe of obligation in Aughnaboy.

Husband/Wife

The bond between husband and wife makes possible a degree of independence from parents, sexual expression, and the raising of children. Marriage is not contracted, however, with the expectation that this new relationship will surpass in affective content the relations with one's own parents and siblings. In fact, the few "love matches" that do exist can create great conflict between a man and his wife's natal family. Consequently, intense affective relations between husband and wife are not only unexpected, they are said to be undesirable, for they carry with them the seeds of discord with the new couple's families of origin. Relations between husband and wife are characterized by quiet, mild, and pleasant behaviour; all that husband and wife expect of each other is the carrying out of his/her duties associated with his/her status cheerfully and with an element of important but unintense affection.

The content of the relationship between husband and wife can usefully be examined in the light of Bott's (1957:53 ff.) discussion of what she calls "segregated conjugal role-relationships." Bott refers to the type of relationship in which the social lives of husband and wife fall into two relatively distinct spheres, where they have "a clear differentiation of tasks and a considerable number of separate interests and activities," and where "they expect to have different leisure pursuits" (*ibid.*). Bott contrasts these segregated relationships with what she calls "joint conjugal role-relationships," where husband and wife "carry out many activities together with a minimum of task differentiation and separation of interests" and they "not only plan the affairs of the family together but also exchange many household tasks and spend much of their leisure time together" (*ibid.*). It is the segregated roles – similar to those Young and Willmott (1957) described for previous generations in Bethnal Green – which best characterize the conjugal relationships in all class strata in Aughnaboy.

The wife's duties revolve around the house and the children: she is responsible for cleaning the house, feeding the family, managing the household expenditure with caution and restraint, comforting the husband, and raising the children in such a way as to preserve the family's "decent name." Her social life is primarily with her children, her parents, and her siblings. Leisure time is spent in endless cups of tea with her mother, joined by her sisters, who gather around the home fire and exchange the gossip of the day as well as the confidences which cement their intimacy. If she has married out of her village, the short distance of ten miles or so still enables her to attend these gatherings at least once or twice a week. When her mother dies, she sits with her sisters in like exchange. When her daughters are grown and married, they will begin to gather at her house throughout the day, perpetuating in this manner the cycle of sociability and emotional succour. She sees her husband at meal times: four times a day if he works in Aughnaboy, one or two a day if he works in Belfast or elsewhere in Ulster, and on weekends or at month's end if he is a fisherman or a sailor. In the evenings, she may sit with her husband and children by her fire and discuss their plans, their needs, and the affairs of the day, or she may repeat her visit to her mother's or her sisters' homes.

The husband's duties consist of the careful management of the family's prestige, providing for the economic and physical well-being of his wife and children, sharing with his wife some of the major decisions regarding the course of their lives, and helping his wife when her authority with the children fails – "your father'll beat ye when he hears about this." The husband is, affectively, a relatively peripheral figure in his family of procreation; his social life is primarily with his workmates during the day and with his brothers and parents in the evenings – dozing by the fire, watching television, drinking in the pubs, or leaning up against the harbour wall to watch the skiffs and trawlers unload their catches. If he is planning a major decision such as emigrating or changing his job, he is as likely to consult his parents and brothers as he is to discuss it with his wife. His wife will expect to be included in the discussions, but she will leave the ultimate decision-making to him. Thus, she will urge – or if she is shrewish, demand – that he leave fishing and come ashore if she lives in his village and is lonely; or, conversely, she may urge him to stay aboard the trawlers if her social needs are met and he is able to earn more at "the fishing" than he would ashore. It is in this sense then that the role-relationships are imperfectly segregated, for the wife expects to be involved in the husband's decision-making: but on any continuum of such relationships, Aughnaboy's husband-wife relationships must approximate a segregated model.

There is some variation in the degree of segregation among the strata: the couples belonging to the highest prestige strata are more likely to share participation in a sport such as golf, and to visit each other's relatives together rather than separately. Generally speaking, however, their spheres of thought and action are relatively distinct and segregated, aside from their children's affairs. A child's progress in school, a son's career, a daughter's behaviour with her boy-friend, these are the matters which commonly bring husband and wife together in Aughnaboy.

Mother/Child
The basic characteristic of Augnaboy's kinship system is what Firth (1956:63) calls "matricentred." The link between mother and child is the strongest for all class strata in matters of affection and influence, and it is the relationship least likely to be disrupted by discord. Mother is the symbol of purity and devotion, of fertility and warmth; mother is the person who sacrificed her life for her children. She is responsible for raising her children, for inculcating in them the basic values of the society, for ensuring that their behaviour is a credit to the family, and for influencing her children to make a prudent choice of marriage partner. In return, the children are expected to lavish her with attention and gifts, to acquiesce to her demands, and to lend economic aid whenever the slightest need arises.

Throughout her life, a mother expects to hold considerable power and influence over her children's affairs. This expectation can and does create conflict with sons who, as they mature and marry, begin to demand a degree of independence. An instance of this is provided by Jock McGonigle, a 40-year-old married fisherman, who was found drinking in Aughnaboy's pub after returning from a voyage. His mother, who disapproved of drinking, and particularly wanted her son to come and talk to her after his absence, went into the pub and loudly demanded that Jock come home. Jock went to avoid a public confrontation, but once home, exploded in rage. He demanded never to be humiliated in public again and "as long as I've me own family and earning me own money, I'll do what I want." His mother, seeing the violence of his emotion, relented. Friction between mother and son is usually resolved by the son's pretending to consent to his mother's wishes, feigning agreement with her desires, and then "going about his own business," maintaining the fiction, for example, that he does not drink and "doesn't hold with drinking" but doing his drinking "on the quiet" in a neighbouring village pub.

In contrast, the relationship between mother and daughter is relatively free of conflict. As in Firth's (1956:63) South Borough, the element of matricentrality is most "characteristically expressed in the relation between a married daughter and her mother," and a daughter remains closely tied to her mother, both physically and emotionally, throughout her life. The degree of this dependence of daughters upon mothers is evidenced in the loss women feel following the death of their mothers: emotional collapse and even nervous breakdowns are not uncommon; on the other hand, such extreme grief is rarely displayed upon the loss of a husband. While both sons and daughters maintain a relationship of intense affection with their mothers throughout their lives, it is the daughters who spend most of their days with their mothers, asking and receiving advice on the best methods of caring for children, feeding babies, treating illnesses and planning meals, as well as discussing the event of the day and sharing the gossip and news regarding local personalities and national problems.

Father/Child

The relations between father and child are marked by superordination and subordination as well as the expectations of love and affection. In Radcliffe-Brown's words (1950:30), "between two proximate generations the relation is normally one of essential inequality, authority, and protective care on the one side, respect and dependence on the other." In Aughnaboy, the father is the symbol of wealth, knowledge, and authority. The father is enjoined to love his child, yet treat him with distance and severity, for "a child should be afraid of his father"; conversely, a child is enjoined to love his father, yet fear and obey him. Social distance is the characteristic quality of the relationship, and, for example, even in middle-age a son will rarely show disrespect by remaining in the same pub his father has entered; and neither will a daughter, single or married, give the slightest hint to her father of her sexual development or her sexual activities with her boy-friends or her husband.

A father's duties towards his children are to enforce discipline in the home when the mother's authority fails, to ensure that his wife is raising the children "properly," and, with his wife to ensure that his children do not sully the family prestige. Primarily, however, the father's duties are to provide for the economic welfare of his children; to ensure that his daughters marry men capable of caring for them. For his sons, he must secure their economic future by either locating them in their apprenticeships or first jobs, or setting them up with their own farms, businesses, or trawlers. His sons will carry on his family name, and represent him and his ancestors to the world and thus declare his worth as a parent and his substance as a man. His economic affairs are thus of crucial importance to them, and it is not expected that sons have much choice in these matters. The father is considered to know best which job will suit his sons' needs and abilities, and it is he who has the necessary contacts to arrange the crucial first job. Jock Quentin, a trawler skipper, had a son Robbie who left school at fifteen when his schoolmaster made it clear that Robbie had no academic abilities. Robbie then wanted to join his father's trawler because it offered quick cash returns in a romantic occupation and because "fishing's in our blood." Robbie's father, however, insisted that Robbie learn a trade "as something to fall back on" if fishing ever became unprofitable, and as an alternative means of employment if Robbie ever decided to take a permanent job on land. After much argument, Robbie relented and Jock used his influence with a carpenter to place Robbie in an apprenticeship. When he had completed four years and received his "papers" as a fully-qualified carpenter, Robbie decided that he preferred a life on land to a life at sea. But Robbie's father insisted that Robbie get his skipper's ticket before making any final decisions, for the trawler would pass to Robbie when his father retired and "ye'd be insane to pass up that much money at the fishing." After intense arguments and threats of leaving home, Robbie relented again and spent six months fishing with his father, then took six weeks off to study for his skipper's ticket examinations. At the age of twenty, Robbie was thus a fully-qualified carpenter and trawler skipper. Robbie had been a dutiful son in obeying his father's wishes against his own desires, and Jock a conscientious father in doing his best to provide for the career of his son.

In return for his father's devotion, a son is expected to treat his father with respect throughout his life, to turn to him for consultation and advice for major decisions, and to provide for him when sickness or old age have reduced his earning capacities. This relationship of continuing social in-

equality is clearly capable of generating conflict between the father's
demands for obedience based on his superior experience and knowledge,
and the son's demands for independence based on his growing maturity. As
the son matures, he wishes to be free to select his own job, his own house,
and to determine for himself the course his life will take: indeed, his
demands for independence become more strident over the years as control
over his own economic life gradually increases.

Fathers who do not own major capital are forced gradually to relinquish
their role in their son's decision-making. But those who do control major
capital subject their sons to their control indefinitely: for their part, the sons
awaiting the inheritance of the estate define their behaviour in terms
of a personal commitment to a family enterprise while continually de-
emphasizing the importance of individual independence. Those who find
the dissonance between the two ideologies of individual independence and
of individual immersion in the group too great, either change their occupations and abandon their share of their father's enterprise, or emigrate; just
as those without capital, whose fathers are too slow to yield domination,
will marry into another village or emigrate.

Sibling/Sibling

The relationships between siblings in Aughnaboy are not like the relations
of "unthinking loyalty" and "simple communism" described by Campbell
for the Sarakatsani (1964:173). Nor, at the other extreme of the European
kinship lexicon, do relations have the flexible and optative character described by Firth (1956) for South Borough in London, where "the moral
obligation is not strongly emphasized" and "siblings may be ignored"
(1956:63). In Aughnaboy, the relations between siblings fall somewhere
between these two extremes. There is a loyalty based on the fundamental
obligations of the nuclear family; but it is a calculating loyalty in that
reciprocity is expected when it is necessary and repayment is expected
when it is feasible, in that mental accounts are kept regarding the exchange
of favours and services, and in that greater prestige accrues to the sibling
who consistently gives more than he receives. In all class strata in Aughnaboy, the moral obligations between siblings are strongly emphasized and
should not be ignored, for to do so would be to risk ostracism from the
family and the contempt of the community.

In strength of obligation and in minimization of choice, the bonds between siblings are second only to the bonds between parents and children.
Siblings are raised together in the same house, share a common social life,
share the prestige of their name, and are identified with one another for
good and for ill by others in the community. They share a fundamental
sense of obligation and responsibility for each other's economic, physical,
and emotional welfare, and are expected to make substantial sacrifices to

ensure this welfare. Ideally, siblings should share everything and "share alike," and they frequently do: they spend their leisure time together, and are obliged to distribute among themselves whatever economic and social opportunities may be available. It is siblings who are expected to stand together in opposition to the rest of the community and to the rest of the world; if one sibling is involved in a feud with a "stranger," then all must withdraw cooperation from the offending person.

Sisters, both before and after marriage, spend most of their leisure time together, learning from their mother and each other how to run a household, discussing in minute detail the experiences of their lives, and drawing upon each other for emotional, and occasionally financial support. Among sisters, favours and services are most freely exchanged: baby-sitting for an evening, caring for the children when the mother is away or in hospital, or lending various household appliances.

Whereas the relationships between sisters are based primarily on the exchange of services and intimate social contact, the relations between brothers are more likely to be predicated on occupational as well as affective and social considerations. Brothers may spend less time together, for their work and interests may take them apart, but they are obliged to help each other on all occasions when the need arises. They share a common name, the prestige of one influences the prestige of the other, they have a mutual interest in their father's property, and they are likely to work together. If they are members of the elite wealth and prestige strata, the intensity of their identification and solidarity is heightened even further by their shared interest in property. If two brothers are skippers, they paint their trawlers the same colours and berth them side by side in the harbour. If it is possible, they build their homes side by side; and if it is not, they still spend their evenings in each other's homes, discussing the price of fish, the quality of rams, or the state of the government. When one is in trouble, they must sacrifice to help, not necessarily out of any higher altruism, but because to fail to do so is to put at risk the reputation of the entire family: thus when the Tague brothers' youngest drank and gambled his business into bankruptcy, his older brothers paid off his debts and his lawyers and set him up in another business, which they privately controlled.

At the same time however, as I shall try to show in subsequent chapters, control of major resources in the family creates additional strains in the relations between brothers, for they must compete for their father's inheritance, and yet they are expected to compromise their own personal economic advance for the welfare of the family.

Contact between brothers and sisters is less frequent and of lesser content than those between siblings of the same sex, and their relations are informed by the awkwardness that characterizes relations between the sexes in Aughnaboy. Nevertheless, relations between brothers and sisters are of considerable warmth and intimacy, and are not complicated by the potential conflict inherent in the relations between brothers. Brothers and sisters grow up together sharing the same joys and sorrows; in adolescence, brothers watch the behaviour of their sisters' boy-friends, and defend them when necessary. When married, brothers and sisters meet almost nightly in the "home place," the home of their parents. If necessary, a brother will find a job for his sister's husband, give her money if she needs it, and visit her on a Sunday if she moves to her husband's village. Siblings stand with parents and children as the closest kin in Aughnaboy, and obligations to assist and defend are strongest within these relationships.

For all the class strata, the family is the fount of loyalty and solidarity, the primary social unit in Augnaboy. Yet no individual is tied to one family only, for each is linked through his parents to their own families of origin and through his siblings to their families of procreation; the nature of these external links is subject to the influence of class-generated dissensus.

The Kindred

5

Aughnaboy's kinship system is a "system" in the sense that there are regularities or patterns in the way in which villagers conceptualize kinship statuses and the rights and duties associated with these statuses. Kinship relations are reckoned through both males and females, and rights are apportioned with a measure of symmetry to both paternal and maternal kin. Through this bilateral web, a man is linked to at least twenty, and sometimes more than one hundred of the nine hundred inhabitants of Aughnaboy. Those they are connected to are often of the same class, for in spite of a degree of social mobility in the village, individuals tend to rise and fall with their families, and there is a marked tendency for a kindred to "find its level"; nevertheless, kinsmen are often from different social strata.

Among Campbell's (1964:42) Sarakatsani, a man will help his "kinsmen and indeed is morally obliged to do so, so long as this assistance does not conflict with the interests of his own family." In Aughnaboy, this assistance is likely to conflict with the familial interests of those in the higher class strata, and it is to their advantage to neither recognize nor honour obligations to extra-familial kin, the kindred. Whereas the ultimate responsibility of all men is to their families, it is only within the lower wealth and authority strata, the masses, that firm moral obligations are recognized and honoured towards all cognatic relatives. In this sense then, class membership alters not only the form of kinship, but also its functions: among the masses, the kindred performs important social and economic functions which it does not perform among the elites.

CLASSIFICATION OF KIN

Categories
Aughnaboy's method of classifying kin can be described in terms of a consensus model, for with minor exceptions, the system of beliefs is shared throughout the village. Several criteria are used to classify kin. At the broadest level, those with whom one has ties of kinship ("friends") or affinity ("friends by marriage" or "connexions") are distinguished from "strangers" or "outsiders" with whom one is not linked by ties of consanguinity or affinity. "Friend" in Aughnaboy means cognate, a usage common among many ancient Teutonic peoples and reported for England as late as the 14th century (Freeman, 1961). "Friends" in Aughnaboy are all

those with whom any degree of consanguineal relationship can be traced,
or even those with whom it is believed that, with the appropriate knowledge, such a relationship could be traced. At the next level, cognates are
distinguished from affines, "friends" from "friends by marriage" or "connexions." Further, cognates themselves are classified into patrilateral kin
("the father's side of the house") and matrilateral kin ("the mother's side
of the house"). Finally, "friends" or cognates are classified on the basis of
genealogical closeness into the two categories of "close friends" and
"far-out friends" – sometimes also called "connexions" – with whom the
exact relationship is unknown or unclear and the obligations minimal.
These distinctions and oppositions based on category and degree are
fundamental to the Aughnaboy kinship system, for it is these which permit
the individual to assess his obligations to a specific kinsman.

"Close friends" form a category of cognates whom it is useful to call the
kindred. In this study, it is a category of persons, not a group, with which
we are dealing when we talk about the kindred. A person's kindred "consists of a set of persons whose relationships are, in various ways, preor-
dained by the fact that they are cognates" (Freeman, 1961). An Iban's
kindred, for example, are those "cognatic kin from whom he can expect
help and to whom he has reciprocal obligations" (ibid.). While Gulliver is
quite right to protest that kindred is in some sense an "artificial analytical
isolate" (1971:15), it is a convenient designator term for individuals who
have a relative in common.

A man's kindred comprise those who have "the one blood," from whom
he inherits not only his prestige (discussed in Chapter 3), but also his
character. If his mother's people are dour, but his father's people cheerful
"droll fellows," then his character may be inherited, in theory, from
"whichever side he's closest to." But in practice, there is a marked
tendency to regard the transmission of character as a sex-linked passage,
and a woman's character is normally attributed to her mother and her
mother's people, while a man's character is attributed to his father and his
father's people.

Range of the Kindred
The range of cognates incorporated in the kindred varies considerably
cross-culturally. According to Freeman (1961), the most commonly reported range is third cousinship, as among the Konkama Lapps, but the
range extends as far as fifth cousins in some bilateral societies. In Aughnaboy, the range of kin recognized normally extends to second cousins
although third cousins are occasionally recognized: even at second cousinship, however, memory of the links begins to dim. A second cousin is
traced through parental links and includes, for example, on the paternal
side, a man's father's father's brother's son – "he's my father's full

cousin''; as well as a man's father's father's brother's son's son – "my father and his father were full cousins"; and the sons of his first ("full") cousins, traced in any direction. Third cousins, reckoned in the same manner, are rarely known and rarely recognized although a term does exist for them; even when they are recognized, no moral obligations are extended to them on the basis of their tenuous kinship links, for they are "too far out."

There is a tendency for this shallow range to be even further restricted in the case of maternal kin. That is, a man's genealogical knowledge normally extends to the first and second cousins on his paternal side, and to many – with a fair number of deficiencies – of his first and second cousins on "the mother's side of the house." Men, women, and children all express the significance of "the name" in their genealogies, of those who share the same patronymic; and a degree of this importance is extended by association to all paternal kin, regardless of whether or not they bear the same patronym. The differentiation of maternal and paternal kin is not what Freeman (1961) calls "situational selectivity"; that is, among the Iban, while kin recognition may in a given case involve forgetting either maternal or paternal kin, for the society, the "structural amnesia" is bilateral. In Aughnaboy, this amnesia is not bilateral – for only one genealogy was recorded in which matrilateral kin out-numbered patrilateral kin, and this was a consequence of a twenty-year-old family feud which resulted in the informant severing all his relations with his patrikin. For the village as a whole, there is a strong patrilateral emphasis in genealogical memory. This is not a function of the geographical distribution of kin, although if "one side of the house" lives thousands of miles away, genealogical knowledge is more likely to be deficient. Neither is this a function of, say, lower prestige of mother's people, for even when this is the case and matrikin are avoided, they are nevertheless usually remembered and recognized. In fact, this patrilateral emphasis in the genealogies is primarily a consequence of the much stronger identification of men with their patrinominal kin, of the over-riding significance of the name, a phenomenon we shall explore later in this chapter.

More generally, Aughnaboy's genealogical range is even shallower and narrower than that of Firth's (1956) South Borough: there the kin universe – cognates and their spouses – varied between 37 and 246 with an average figure of 146, whereas in Aughnaboy, 89 is the average in a range between 15 and 241. Generation depth too is extremely shallow. The average recorded depth in the collected genealogies was 4.6 generations, a middle-aged man being likely to remember two generations above and one or two generations below his own.

An additional characteristic of genealogical knowledge in Aughnaboy is that each generation sloughs off a section of the knowledge of the previous generation: it forgets, or in Sarakatsani terms, "throws away" the cousins and the grandparents its fathers know. Each generation then traces its genealogy to its grandparents, and the previous generations remembered by their fathers are forgotten. In this manner, grandparents' siblings and their children – great-uncles and second cousins in Aughnaboy's parlance – are gradually removed from each generation's cognizance. Nevertheless, even though the links which connect a man to his grandfather's siblings' children and grand-children are forgotten, he often knows many of those who are his second cousins because he remembers that "his father and my father were full cousins." In like manner, third cousins are occasionally recognized, for they can be the children of a man's second cousins, or possibly "his father and mine were second cousins."

Terminology

Kinship terminology clearly expresses the main features of the Aughnaboy kinship system which are 1) the isolation of the family as the centre of the villager's universe, and 2) for most men, the extension of moral obligations and love to one's kindred according to the degree of closeness of the relationship. Terms which are used for relations within the family of origin and the family of procreation are not carried over to other collateral kinsmen as they are in many societies with, say, classificatory terminologies. Kinship terminology describes the approximate genealogical relationship between two men, and indicates the strength of their mutual "obligement." Kin terms are used only if speaking directly to parents: "mummy" and "daddy"; to grandparents: "granny" and "grandad"; and occasionally, to uncles and aunts.

Cousin terms are described in fractions, and closely follow the villager's perceptions of genealogical closeness and degree of moral obligation. No distinctions in terminology are made between patrilateral or matrilateral cousins, or between parallel or cross-cousins. Closest of all cousins are "double cousins," the product of the extremely rare brother and sister exchange for which only one case was recorded. Closest of all cousins for most people are "full cousins"; that is, first cousins, the children of a man's parents' siblings, who are "just one by a brother and sister." Second cousins are called "half-cousins"; they are "getting further out," and are at the periphery of a man's kindred. Although half-cousins include, in theory, the grandchildren of a man's grandparents' siblings, genealogical depth is normally so shallow that these are generally not recognized, and half-cousins normally refer to the children of one's full cousins. Beyond the range of effective kin incorporated in the kindred are third cousins who are called "quarter cousins"; but they are rarely recognized and "once you get to that point, there's no friendship at all."

The terminological system could be called a classificatory one, not in the classic anthropological sense in which terms applied to lineal relatives can also be applied to collateral kin, but rather in the sense that there is an inverse relationship between the "closeness" of a given relationship and the number of alternative kin types which can be subsumed under the single term. That is, the closest relationships tend to be assigned a single term which can be applied to no others, whereas the "further out" the relationship, the greater number of kin types which are classified under a single term. Full cousin, for example, incorporates eight different kin types and half-cousin incorporates thirty-two separate kin types. This, in itself, delineates the degree of importance assigned to different ranges of kindred. Within a man's family of origin and procreation, the terminology is purely descriptive, but once beyond this range of family, a single term incorporates a progressively increasing number of kin types which reflects with no little accuracy the significance accorded them.

In sum then, there is a shared, or consensual, classificatory system in which the range of cognates who are remembered is normally traced two generations above the individual and to second cousins; it is this category which I have called the kindred.

MORAL OBLIGATIONS WITHIN THE KINDRED

Whereas the classificatory system is largely shared by all class strata, the recognition of moral obligations towards members of the kindred is not a matter of consensus among the villagers. Here, differential access to resources generates conflicting interests which can be analysed only in terms of a dissensus model. This dissensus occurs at several points in the structure: in the degree of isolation of the family from the kindred, the strength of obligations to members of the kindred, and in the frequency and content of interaction.

Relations between kindred are more than simply the exchange of genealogical information. In a village such as this where there are no large-scale corporate kin groups, the kindred is the only unit beyond the family in which the qualities of trust and loyalty reside, and among kindred there are moral obligations of a priority second only to those held towards the family. There is what Freeman (1961) calls a "special morality arising from the recognition of common descent." Kindred are obliged to lend help and support in specific situations, normally social or economic. That is, while there is no ancestor-focused descent group into which he is recruited by birth, he has a category of relatives traced from himself upon whom he can make claims. Further, even though there is no definite prescription for an X type of kinsman to perform Y action in Z situation, there is a generalized obligation to assist a kinsman when one is called upon to do so and, if the person is very close, help is offered before it is solicited. To give succour during sickness, to lend labour to a farmer uncle at harvest time, to find a job or lend money to a cousin temporarily out of work, in general to "stick up more for your blood relatives than for the outsider," these are the obligations which tie kindred to one another. The recognition of their common descent, the belief that they share "the one blood," create bonds of loyalty, trust, and cooperation between them which is rarely possible between two unrelated men.

All other obligations and duties should be subordinated to the needs of one's kindred. An example of this occurred when a hurricane was forecast to hit the Irish coast within six or seven hours. The two types of fishermen who use Aughnaboy harbour came into conflict. The large trawler men wanted the harbour sealed off immediately with the protective booms in order to secure their vessels from damage during the hurricane. On the other hand, the inshore skiff fishermen insisted that the harbour entrance be left open for a few additional hours to enable them to fish for the morning before the hurricane reached Aughnaboy. At this point the Harbour Master intervened: being the mother's brother of three of the trawler skippers, he threatened to call the police and involve the skiff fishermen in a court action unless the harbour was sealed off. After much shouting and threatening, the protective booms were lowered into place and the harbour sealed off. Whereas the inshore skiff fishermen complained that the Harbour Master had no rights over the booms sealing off the harbour, they at no time questioned the legitimacy of his decision nor his obligation to support his kinsmen, and they took no action following the incident.

Gradation of Obligation
The kindred, however, is not an undifferentiated block. Obligations of equal strength are not extended to all members of a man's kindred, but are determined according to the "closeness" of genealogical relationship and the kinship category, with a gradual reduction in the strength of these obligations occurring as one nears the group's peripheries. The individual feels obliged to perform acts for a brother's son that he would not perform for a full cousin and so on.

There is dissensus between the classes with regard to the obligations which are recognized for the different degrees of closeness. Whereas members of the lower strata recognize obligations to full cousins and even to half-cousins, the elites are continually de-emphasizing the obligations towards cousins: "I don't think you have a duty to cousins"; "you'd recognize him, he's a cousin of mine, but I don't think it goes further than that." The significance of this de-emphasis of kindred will emerge more fully in subsequent chapters, but it should be clear that it is in the interests of the elites to emphasize the nuclear family at the expense of the kindred, and to downgrade the significance of members of the wider kindred: "second cousins are just a little step above people you'd meet on the streets."

In addition to genealogical distance, kinship category is an important mechanism for apportioning obligation by all the villagers. By "kinship category," I refer to the strong patrilateral bias in this otherwise bilateral kinship system. Few societies are perfectly bilateral: affection, identification, and the complex of political, ritual, social, and economic obligations often tend to be asymmetrical in their distribution. In Aughnaboy, patrinominal kin – those who bear the same surname – and by association, all patrilateral kin (including those, such as father's married sister, who do not bear the same surname) are clearly distinguished from matrilateral kin. Major items of capital are transmitted largely between patrinominal kin; economic favours are most likely to be exchanged between patrinominal kin as when two patrilateral parallel cousins assist each other in finding work; and membership in the various Protestant denominations is transmitted through males, women converting to the denomination and church of their husbands upon marriage.

Affective ties may in a given case be fully bilateral – "I feel the same for both sides" – or strongly patrilateral, or matrilateral, but for the village as a whole, individuals are as likely to express the same love for both "sides of the house" as they are for patrilateral kin. Yet the identification of males is most likely to be with their patrinominal kin; a man is, like his father, "a McKibbin." "I'm a McKibbin, and coursing through the veins of another McKibbin is the same blood." Generally, a man feels stronger obligations to his patrinominal kinsmen: you "would go quickest to your father's side if you wanted help;" "in a fight, your father's people would help you more." In Young and Willmott's (1957) Bethnal Green, it is women who act as the pivotal links in maintaining kinship relations; a woman focuses her social relations upon her mother; this, in turn, structures the kinship universe for men as well. But in Aughnaboy, there is a strong element of unisexuality which informs all social interaction. If in Bethnal Green, the mother-daughter tie is the primary kinship link and the link which structures the remainder of relations between kinsmen, in Aughnaboy, the association between patrinominal kin – men who bear the same name – is just as important. The remarks of one stone mason illustrate these values: "Boys cling more to the father's side, and girls more to the mother's side. The boys would be with the father visiting his people, and the girls would stay at home with the mother, and with the mother's people. A boy'd see the same in the father's brother as in the father, they'd be much in the same line of work, the same interests, their background would be the same."

From childhood, this sexual differentiation of activity begins to dominate their social interaction: a young boy will accompany his father and his father's brothers to the harbour to check the fish prices and to comment on the corruption and immorality of the fish buyers, or to the livestock auctions to watch his father perform and haggle and so learn from him the requirements for his own future work. A young girl, on the other hand, will remain at home with her mother, or accompany her to her mother's sisters or parents. Further, adult work spheres reinforce this unisexual identification, for women belong to the domestic sphere and they must depend upon other women for the exchange of services and knowledge important to them – a situation made more difficult for those women who have married into the village, but still possible for them now with the widespread use of cars and buses; men, on the other hand, whose occupational sphere lies in the outside world, must depend upon other men for help and it is towards their patrinominal kin that they are most likely to turn.

Finally there is the matter, already much alluded to, of the *name*. There is a community of interest for which the name is a symbol, and this common interest links all who bear the same name in a bond of quasi-mystical intensity – an intensity whose roots are nonetheless firmly secured in economic reality. It is those who share the same name who will inherit major capital, for a man without children will leave his farm or trawler to his brother's son who shares his name rather than give it to a sister's son who would "take it out of the name." This knowledge links a woman closer to her husband's people than he is to her people, for the future welfare of her sons will depend upon the grace of her husband's people. Those who share the same name are perceived as one unit by the community, for they are assigned a common social personality and a shared level of prestige. In order to maintain their social honour, they must live up to the obligations which bind kindred one to another. Kindred must help one another, and particularly one's patrinominal kinsmen, not only because of a moral obligation, but also because if one allows a kinsman's position to slip too far, then "the whole name would be dragged under."

Selection of Kin

As important as the notion of gradation of obligation based on genealogical distance and kinship category, is the notion of *choice* inherent in kindred relations. The kindred is a flexible organization which presents the individual with a wide range of choice, a range of optative relationships. As Freeman (1961) phrases it, "in the absence of any binding descent principle, it is possible for a man to accentuate as he pleases or as it suits his special interest." The Aughnaboy system has this optative character, for ties through both or either parent are always available as potential points of attachment, and "either or both may be chosen according to circumstances." Among Freeman's (*op. cit.*) Iban, a man's kindred consists of a group of people with whom he can by right attach himself when it suits his needs or interests, and it frequently happens that "a man's closest ties are by choice with 'distant' rather than 'near' members of his kindred." In Aughnaboy, a man is also free to demand favours or services from anyone with whom he can claim "close friendship." If it happens that his uncles are in no position to help him – if, for example, they work in other occupations, or if they are very poor – then he can ask a favour of a full cousin instead (or even, occasionally, a half-cousin). Tommy McLandress has a permanent berth on his full cousin's trawler, his father's brother's son, which he claimed on the basis of his kinship ties. His cousin is thus of major importance to him economically, whereas his uncles and nephews are of relatively minor importance.

But this is not to suggest that members of the kindred fall into two categories: those who are utilized and those who are not or, in Firth's (1956:45) terms, effective and non-effective, respectively. For the situation is in a constant state of flux: a man may use his cousin for one purpose and a nephew for another; and a cousin whose services have not been used for years may suddenly be in a position to help a man through a change in either of their circumstances. Each person in a man's kindred is a potential source of aid, and some may be utilized regularly and others rarely if at all.

ROLES IN THE KINDRED

The kindred can also be usefully examined as a network of roles. But although the conceptualization is shared throughout the population, dissensus generated by the class structure becomes apparent in certain situations.

In Aughnaboy, the relations between grandparent and grandchild are said to be characterized by affection and indulgence. The grandparents are the most honoured of all kinsmen for they are the source of a man's kindred and the parents of his parents. Relations between these alternate generations are not restrained by problems of authority and obedience. These two alternate generations are involved in relations not of superordination and subordination but "of simple friendliness and solidarity and something approaching social equality," (Radcliffe-Brown, 1950). The grandparent is expected to indulge every whim of the grandchild; in return, the grandchild is expected to reciprocate with lavish affection and honour and, in later life, with care and concern which take the form of regular visits, running errands, and the provision of comforts such as television sets which make their grandparents' remaining time more pleasant. Thus, every night Sheila helps her grandmother who is blind and deaf into bed; McKeague helps his grandfather with the work on his farm, and brings the occasional gift of mackerel or "clams" (scallops) which his grandfather adores. The fact that a man's father's parents bear the same name as his own makes him rather closer in the public's identification with them, but the quality of the social relations between him and his two sets of grandparents is little affected by this difference. They are his oldest living kinsfolk who lavished him with love and care during his childhood; he makes few, if any, distinctions between them, and an infinite number of allowances for them. While the matter of the name means that it is more likely for him to inherit property from his paternal grandparents than from his maternal ones, the preference for transmitting property one generation below the holder normally rules the grandchild out of this inheritance, and his relations with his grandparents are thus not constrained by the prospect of inheritance.

The relations between uncles/aunts and nephews/nieces are also characterized by affection and indulgence and in this respect, they are similar to the relations between grandparents and grandchildren. Here, however, the patrinominal principle intrudes more strongly, and a distinction is made between mother's brothers and father's brothers. Favours may be exchanged between a mother's brother and his nephew, but it is generally expected that the primary relationship will be a social or expressive one of affection and warmth. Maternal uncles do not transmit property to a man, and their relationship is uncomplicated by this factor. In contrast, a young man's father's brother who bears the same name and the same prestige is most likely to assist his father in deciding his career and in obtaining his first job. Additionally, for those who own major capital, what is perhaps the most critical element in their relationship is that the nephew is his father's brother's prospective heir if the paternal uncle has no children of his own. In such cases, nephews (patrilateral parallel cousins) and siblings will compete for the favour of their uncle, bringing him his meals from their own kitchens, visiting him in the long evenings, posting his letters and running his errands – services which are expected to endear him more to one nephew than to another.

Relations between aunts and their nephews and nieces are not complicated by this element of the patronym for, unless the aunts are unmarried, they do not bear the same surname. Further, aunts as women are confined primarily to the domestic sphere, and are unlikely to be independently wealthy unless they have inherited "fortunes" of their own, in which case, they will tend to "favour" those who share their surname. Thus, relations between aunts and their nephews and nieces are primarily social. Another element here is that social relations between parents' siblings and siblings' children tend to be unisexual in nature: females are more likely to engage in long-term social relations with their aunts, and particularly their mother's sisters. Conversely, men are more likely to engage in enduring social and economic relations with their father's brothers.

Finally, there is the phenomenon that relations between parents' siblings and siblings' children are not entirely reciprocal, and tend to change over time. A young unmarried aunt or uncle will "make a great fuss" over his first nephews or nieces, and spend considerable time with them, taking them for drives or walks, indulging them liberally, and delighting in his new role. As time passes and he himself marries and raises his own children, his interest in his constantly growing number of nephews and nieces tends to decrease. This tendency is not shared by the nieces and nephews themselves who continue to esteem their parents' only siblings. In the case of males and their patrilateral uncles, there is often the delicate matter of prospective inheritance to sustain interest and encourage interaction; then it is the nephews who begin to dance attendance on their uncles.

Relations between male patrilateral parallel cousins are complicated by class-generated conflict; as I have suggested above, they, along with siblings must compete with one another for a childless uncle's capital. Additionally, patrilateral parallel cousins share the same name and all that goes with it and so distinctions are made between them and all other cousins. Thus, among full cousins, McTavish is closer to his father's brother's son than to his other cousins, and he is more likely to volunteer assistance when the situation requires it than he is with his patrilateral cross-cousins or any of his matrilateral cousins. Yet, here too, the distinction is one of degree rather than one of kind, and expectations of loyalty and support extend to all cousins.

The matter of genealogical distance is equally significant. As I have already mentioned, full (first) cousins are "just one by a brother and sister" for the majority of the population, and the obligations which unite them are similar but not as strong as those which unite siblings. Cousins are not expected to visit each other regularly in adulthood, but they are likely to be thrown together in childhood when they accompany their parents on almost daily visits if they live nearby and Sundays and summer fortnights if they live further away.

Among the masses, full cousins are expected to lend aid in times of difficulty, to be given preference (beyond the family and nephews/uncles) in hiring, and in general to give priority to assisting one another in their social and economic lives. With half (second) cousins, the blood is "twice diluted" in marriage, and the closeness of their relationship and the strength of their obligations are correspondingly reduced. Half cousins are a "breaking point" at which villagers "begin to get away from friendship." Half-cousins are much less likely to see each other regularly in childhood, the affairs of their parents are less likely to be discussed in intimate detail by their own parents, and they do not grow up with the same attachments and associations which bind full cousins to one another. Nevertheless, the bond is recognized and if an individual has no conflicting obligations to closer kinsmen, he is expected to lend aid and support to his half cousins when possible, particularly when they bear the same surname.

Quarter (third) cousins are what the terminology suggests, and the blood is so diluted that they are "no friends at all really." It is rare for people to know who their quarter-cousins are – the grandchildren of their full cousins, the children of their half-cousins and their parents' half-cousins –

and even when they do know, they are beyond the boundaries of the kindred; they are "far out friends." "The granny might tell you about quarter-cousins, but the younger people wouldn't know about them." Here the fact of quarter-cousinship, or even of bearing the same surname, is a matter of what is essentially historical interest to the villagers, beyond the dominion of "obligement."

FUNCTIONS OF THE KINDRED

Functionally, the kinship system is a major feature of Augnaboy. The fact that there is a moral obligation for kindred to support one another means that a mechanism is created for the mobilization of individuals for specific purposes. In Augnaboy, differential class interests create a functional dissensus in that different strata's kindreds vary in their performance of different functions. Thus it is that social and economic functions of the kindred are exceedingly important for the masses, but of minor significance for the elites. Conversely, the religious and political functions of the kindred are of greater significance for the elites than they are for the masses.

In the *economic* sector, Aughnaboy is very different from urban Britain where "kinship does not play much part in the economic and occupational structure," where people do not have to depend upon their relatives for access to some means of earning a living, and where "there are few economic ties and obligations among extra-familial kin" (Bott, 1971:124). In Aughnaboy, among the lower strata, a man's family and kindred are of vital importance to him as potential sources of economic aid. This is not to suggest that there are economic groups to which the individual is automatically assigned by virtue of his descent; neither are there clear-cut jural obligations for an individual to contribute his labour or capital to one man or group rather than to another. On the contrary, every individual is subject to a variety of obligations and influences, and he chooses that course which appears most advantageous to him. But in Aughnaboy, where men in the lower strata rely on jobs with uncertain and insecure tenure, it is the support of their kinsmen that in the long-run is most likely to prove to be to their advantage. Thus, for skilled labourers and fishermen for example, family and kindred constitute a network of alliance and an important avenue for the exchange of information and influence regarding new and better jobs. Kindred also assist in placing one's children in their careers, for providing credit in times of emergency, and providing avenues for social mobility. Men of the lower strata, then, are not yielding unthinkingly to the demands of the kinship ideology when they help their kin: on the contrary, they are performing rational and logical acts, for they are banking favours and ensuring that reciprocal aid will be offered them if and when they are in a similar position of need.

For members of the upper strata, however, kindred do not occupy a central place in economic affairs, and do not provide an important favour-bank. Rather, economic connections with kin are regarded as a hindrance and an "awkwardness" – except in the early stages of the formation of a new enterprise (see Ch. 8 for more details). For the elites, then, the interests of their class positions generate very different needs, which in turn necessitate the adoption of a different set of values and beliefs regarding the economic significance of kin.

In the *social* sector, family and kindred are of vital significance in a number of ways. Kinsmen are important for it is with them that one identifies most closely and is, in turn, identified by the community. Men share a common social personality and often their prestige with their close kinsmen – especially with their patrinominal kin – and it is through family and kindred that the individual finds his place in society. Family and kindred are also important sources of social support. Close kin are the major, and sometimes the only, source of aid and sustenance during the ceremonies which mark a man's passage through the crises of birth, marriage, and death; it is close kin who are most closely touched by the sorrow and joy which accompany these occasions. One turns to kin for help during domestic crises such as hospitalization, for support in disputes with non-kin, and in confrontations with judicial authority.

Finally, family and kindred are of vital significance in *social interaction*. For the masses, one's friends are normally one's "friends," and it is kinsmen, not "strangers," who visit in each other's homes, share leisure hours, and confide their intimate thoughts, desires, and fears. The elites, however, must seek their friendships beyond the boundaries of their genealogies, with "chums" and in voluntary associations (cf. Leyton, 1975). But for most of the villagers, the family is the centre of social life. It is also among close kin that moral consensus is reached in that the behaviour of others can be evaluated openly and a consensus of moral judgement determined. Only here can one discuss invidiously the affairs of another unrelated family, for to do so with non-kin would be to risk giving serious offense; only here can a man, without fear of retribution, pass judgement on the affairs of his fellow men, knowing that his remarks will not be passed beyond the intimate circle.

The two cases given below provide illustrations of the differences in social interaction between the social classes. One week in the life of McMaster, a carpenter, illustrates the form and content of social interaction between kin among the lower class strata. He spent Sunday visiting his father and mother in Drumkil, sitting by their fire at tea discussing the events of the past few weeks, their plans and ambitions, and the gossip of the day. On Monday, having previously been approached by his father's brother, a fisherman whose son did not want to go "to the fishing," he hired his cousin as an apprentice carpenter, thereby guaranteeing his cousin a career that is much sought after and difficult to secure. On Tuesday, his mother's father, a farmer, asked him for help on his farm and McMaster spent all day there, baling hay and transferring the bales from the fields to the barn. On Thursday, he decided to trade in his Mini for a larger car. He went to his father for advice and he suggested a car dealer he knew in Belfast who would give him a "special deal" on a car if he mentioned that his father knew the dealer. McMaster then asked his brother, who considered himself knowledgeable about cars, to help him buy a new Ford. Then, needing a trailer bar installed, he bought the bar and had his father's brother, a machinist, install it on the car's rear bumper. Finally, on Saturday, he finished repainting his mother's sister's kitchen, a favour which his mother had previously asked him to perform.

For the elites, however, interaction with the kindred is much less frequent and of less content. These owners of large firms and professionals regard the exchange of economic favours as embarrassing and the offering of advice presumptious: "for troubles of a certain nature, they would go to a solicitor or an auctioneer; the tendency now is to seek qualified advice." Additionally, elite values exclude performing "menial" tasks such as repainting a kitchen, as they are considered beneath their station and could compromise their dignity. Indeed, members of these strata tend to disavow any knowledge or competence in these matters, invariably hiring men for these purposes. Finally, the elites may have kindred in much lower strata, and contact with them could emphasize the ambiguous social reputation of their "blood" and compromise their own prestige. Those who control hiring also take pains to avoid many of their kindred because they are continually importuned to hire kin and it is against all their economic interests to do so (see Ch. 8).

As a result of these factors, the elites avoid close contact with kindred. A week in the life of McKibbin, an Aughnaboy stone yard owner illustrates this process and contrasts with the example given above: the sum total of his contact with extra-familial kin was once on Wednesday, when he attended the funeral of a full cousin in Drumkil, and once on Sunday afternoon, when he had his mother's sister to his house for tea. His evenings are occupied primarily with his memberships in voluntary associations such as the British Stone Federation, the Masons, and the Golf Club; it is here and with his family that his social life takes place. "Apart from the organizations I'm tied up with, I'm content to sit in my own home."

In the *political* sector, kindred are of some significance in power relations within the community (cf. Leyton, 1966). A man's kindred are expected to support him in his feuds and to withdraw cooperation from anyone who has seriously and unequivocally injured him – for to slight one member of the kindred is to slight them all. Secondly, political affiliation is inherited: a man is by birth a member or, at least, supporter of the Conservative and Unionist Party, and to be a Protestant is to be committed irrevocably to the maintenance of Northern Ireland's political union with Great Britain. More important, a man is expected to use his position – if he has one – in the political bureaucracy for the benefit of his kin, to ensure that his powers advance his family and kindred. In order to do so, he would make it possible for them to obtain a council house which would otherwise be unobtainable, or process a form with a minimum of delay, or grant building permission when it might not otherwise be granted.

Manipulation of the political bureaucracy is more possible for the elites as they are more likely to stand at elections and receive political appointments. But, in general, this is a set of beliefs shared by all and, given a degree of delicacy, the individual does not have to compromise his own advancement in order to assist his kin.

In the *ritual* sector, kinsmen are significant in the sense that a man takes his religious denomination from his father, and a woman from her husband. More important, a man must maintain doctrinal solidarity with his kin, and religious convictions must at all times be subordinated to kinship loyalties for, as I have already suggested, a man is endangering the social position of all his kin if he allows his religious beliefs to grow heretical. To convert to another denomination is to insult one's kinsmen, to lower their esteem in the eyes of the community, and to risk the loss of future support. Additionally, while all men use their ritual performance as a public statement of their spirituality and as a means to raise their public esteem, the elites must be particularly conscious of this, since it is they who are nominated to the Elders of the Churches, and who must officiate at many of the churches' "social" functions.

CONFLICT WITHIN THE KINDRED

The conclusion to be drawn from the preceding pages is not that members of a kindred dwell in a state of mystical concord, or that moral obligations are always fulfilled. This is not the case. As I have tried to show earlier in this study and elsewhere (Leyton, 1966), the intimate bonds between close cognates are capable of generating considerable conflict. The conflict is especially intense with patrinominal kin – those for whom the bonds are purported to be the closest and the loyalties the strongest. The strength of the bonds between members of a kindred are not an illusion; but conflict of interest is most likely to arise between patrinominal kin, and especially those who own major items of capital. Men with trawlers or farms to pass on to their sons or nephews exercise the greatest authority and arouse the most intense rebellions – rebellions which sometimes end in the severing of all relations between uncle and nephew or father and son. In this manner, young Heaney, "driven half-mad" by his father's refusal to grant him any autonomy, and "bored to death" with endless hours working for a pittance in his uncle's business, severed all relations with his kindred.

But for the majority of the population, where the passage of major capital items is not an issue, relations within the kindred can be characterized by trust and affection. It is therefore not surprising that only a small proportion of Aughnaboy's disputes occur between kindred other than patrinominal kin, for there is little authority conflict, competition, or rivalry; also, affiliation with other kinsmen provides support and affection, but does not place the individual under stringent or conflicting obligations. This is partially because of the conventions of conduct which bid a man behave towards his kindred with cheerfulness and friendliness; partially because if a man clashes with a kinsman, he need merely avoid his company; and partially because, knowing that alienating kindred is risking the loss of a fundamental source of support, a man will make sacrifices to ensure the harmony and cordiality of his relations with his kin.

SUMMARY

I have tried to give a description of the kinds of relations associated with the kindred in Aughnaboy, and of the differential ideology and behaviour which is generated by membership in different class strata. For the elites, the complications inherent in social and economic relations with kindred lead to a de-emphasizing of the kindred and a stressing of the family's fundamental significance and its isolation from the kindred. But among the masses, the family is seen as a less isolated unit, as a group which is embedded in the wider kindred; notions of "the one blood" provide the rationale for extending moral obligations to members of the kindred. For them, it is the ego-focused kindred which, with the family, provide the most powerful network of support and alliance. Unless the bonds which unite them are broken by death or emigration, they are of great strength and longevity, and provide channels for aid and support second only to the family.

Marriage and Affinity

6

Marriage in Aughnaboy is a religious sacrament which unites two individuals, an institution which provides for the legitimization, succour, and socialization of children, and a contract of alliance which establishes new rights and obligations between the kin of bride and groom. As such, a marriage is not just the concern of the couple, but also of the kinsmen of the bride and groom, and it is influenced by class-generated variables. These issues will be examined below; at the moment, our concern is to describe the factors which shape Aughnaboy's marriage patterns.

To remain unmarried in Aughnaboy is not to achieve the state of grace through chastity often attributed to Irish peasant society (cf. Connell, 1968); nor is it, on the other hand, "the admission of some grave moral or physical deficiency" as it is among Campbell's (1964:150) Sarakatsani. The inhabitants of Aughnaboy are subject to some of the constraints which condemned one quarter of the population of County Clare (Arensberg and Kimball, 1940) to a life of celibacy (approximately one-tenth of the population of Aughnaboy remain unmarried), but the expectation in Aughnaboy is clearly that every man and woman should marry.

What is at issue is whom they should marry, and when this marriage should take place. Whom they should marry is a complex matter in a village without the arranged marriages typical of much of European peasant society (cf. Arensberg and Kimball, 1940; Campbell, 1964; Stirling, 1965) where marriage is a matter for negotiation between the parents of the bride and groom, and where the couple themselves have little, if any, influence in the actual decision-making. In Aughnaboy there are no matchmakers, no dowries, no formal and institutionalized arrangements for contracting marriages, and there are no clear-cut prescriptions dictating whom the individual should marry.

There is a tendency in anthropology to assume that in societies where prescriptive or preferential marriage rules are lacking, the choice of marriage partners is random and therefore not a matter for structural inquiry. But this is not the case in Aughnaboy: marriage is by no means a random combination, and there are, in fact, a host of constraints and incentives which structure an individual's choice of mate.

MARRIAGE PROHIBITIONS

There are several important prohibitions and avoidances which structure mate selection in Aughnaboy. Kinship conceptions regulate the first set of prohibitions: the Government of Northern Ireland and the Church of Ireland specifically prohibit marriage between members of a nuclear family, between all lineal relatives and collaterals to the second degree, and to one's siblings' spouses, one's parents' siblings and their spouses, and one's dead wife's siblings. These prohibitions are sanctioned by law and the courts, and by the power available to the Church of Ireland to discipline and expel its own members.

Local custom further restricts the range of mates by strongly discouraging marriage between persons with whom bonds of consanguinity can be traced, whatever the degree of relationship. This is a consequence of the biological beliefs, already referred to, that physical damage such as mental deficiency, insanity, and physical deformities can be done to the issue of a marriage between kin. These beliefs refer primarily to procreative activity between close kin, but are extended by association to any range of kin and even to those who are suspected of being related, such as fellow villagers. For, "if you went back far enough, everybody in the village would be related."

Thus it is that young people of courting age prefer to avoid liaisons with those from the same village, "explaining" their behaviour through claims that the opposite sex in their own village is "desperate" and uninteresting, whereas those from other villages and townlands are "different," "better-looking," and more interesting. Connell (1962) has referred to this sentiment as "antipathy to forming a romantic attachment with the girl one has known since the dummy dribbled from her mouth." In practice, those of courting age seek their mates at the country dances held in Orange Halls all over the county, and particularly in the Perrins. The majority of attachments are formed there. Those in the highest prestige strata conduct their courting elsewhere, primarily through the universities and private schools, finding their "social equals" in the institutions which link them to the wider society.

In spite of the prevailing social arrangements and beliefs which militate against intra-village marriages, a substantial minority of marriages do take place between individuals both of whom "belong" to Aughnaboy (26 percent in a stratified sample). There are distinct advantages to such matches for the couple, providing it can be shown that there are no kinship links between them. Intra-village marriages offer both boy and girl the opportunity to remain in their natal village near their families, and neither of them is forced to sacrifice daily social interaction with their families. In fact, however, the majority of marriages occur with people from other villages or townlands, but within the Perrin region: of a sample of thirty-eight marriages in which at least one of the couple "belonged" to Aughnaboy, ten found their mates in Aughnaboy, twenty had spouses who came from somewhere within the Perrin region, four came from within the

County but outside the Perrins, and four spouses came from outside the County.

Those related through the bonds of affinity do not often marry, but the reason for this is not the same as the Sarakatsani prohibition where even the suggestion of such a match is met with "shocked incredulity" (Campbell, 1964:145). The rarity of marriage in Aughnaboy between those related through affinal "connexions" (only one case was recorded: two brothers married two sisters) is a function of the incongruity between the trust of kinsmen and the possibility of sexual interest. That is, relations of trust and attitudes of loyalty are expected to some degree between affines, and this trust and loyalty lessen the possibility of a sexual association in Aughnaboy where sex is regarded as a dangerous, and even an evil force. Thus, no objections would be raised to the marriage of a man to, say, his brother's wife's sister, but she is almost unconsciously removed from the range of potential mates because of the sexual propriety that is expected between them. In addition, a judicious person will contract an alliance with a new kin group rather than duplicate an existing affinal link.

Religion is the second major structural feature which limits mate selection. It functions at two levels: the total prohibition of marrying Catholics, and the strong avoidance of marrying into other denominational levels. First, Protestants must marry Protestants, and even the suggestion of deviation from this norm is met with shocked incredulity. Children are raised on tales and songs of "traitors" who married "Papishes," and the social arrangements described in chapter 2 make it highly unlikely that such liaisons would develop. Only one case of a match between Protestant and Catholic occurred during my research in Aughnaboy, and a police escort was necessary at the wedding ceremony to protect the couple from the wrath of their families.

Finer discriminations than this are made, however, and within the Protestant community, only a limited form of inter-denominational marriage is encouraged. Essentially, villagers do not compromise their position in the prestige hierarchy, and for the members of the established denominations (Church of Ireland, Presbyterians and Methodists), marriage with the lower prestige fundamentalist denominations is strongly discouraged. Indeed, opportunities for "courting" members of the fundamentalist denominations are few, for most matches are made at the "socials" and dances held throughout the Perrins; members of the fundamentalist denominations do not "hold with" dancing, and are thus unlikely to meet the others in situations where courting could be initiated.

Further, marriages between members of the different fundamentalist denominations are regarded as unusual or unfortunate: whereas it is quite normal and acceptable for a high prestige Presbyterian to marry a high prestige Methodist, it is a moral capitulation and a spiritually dangerous act

for a Baptist to marry a Plymouth Brethren or a Presbyterian, for each of
the fundamentalist denominations believe that members of all other denominations and religions will "surely go to Hell." For a Presbyterian or
Church of Ireland member to marry a member of a fundamentalist denomination is to consign his children and himself to a lower social level and to
compromise accordingly the prestige of his entire family; and for a
Plymouth Brethren or another fundamentalist to marry a member of any
other denomination is to risk consigning himself and his children to the
"everlasting fires of Hell and Damnation." Thus members of the established denominations marry freely amongst themselves, while members of
the fundamentalist denominations marry only members of the same denomination.

MARRIAGE PREFERENCES

Even though there are no prescriptions to indicate whether a man should or
must marry a classificatory kinsman or a member of a certain village, there
is one important set of preferences which guides an individual's selection of
mate; here I refer to the principle of prestige maximization. All adults are
enjoined to maintain or increase their level of prestige: in order to achieve
this through the institution of marriage, individuals prefer to marry those of
equal or superior prestige; and their parents are obliged to ensure that such
behaviour is forthcoming. When Betty displayed an interest in a young man
who was her social inferior, her parents disparaged the boy in her presence,
ridiculed her interest in him, and made him feel "awkward" and unwel-
come in their house. But when Betty began courting the socially prominent
Noel, the parents' strategy was reversed: Noel was invited into the home,
offered the use of their car, and lavishly praised both in public and in
private.

To reinforce these strategies, stories are told and re-told in the village of
those who have ignored the advice of their parents, and married those
"beneath them." Another story was the following: "Maggie wanted to
marry Sam for years, but his mother wouldn't hear of it. She said Maggie
wasn't good enough for her wee Sam – and who would take care of her if
Sam went off and got married? Finally, Maggie got pregnant so old Sam had
to marry her; you could hear his mother screaming a mile away. Then they
moved into Sam's house with the mother. Maggie and the mother couldn't
get along at all, and Sam's sisters backed the mother. Everything Maggie
did was wrong. They used to fight all the time until finally they just stopped
talking to each other. It went on like that till the old mother died."

Stories such as these make effective sanctions. The young man or
woman looking for a person to court is anxious to avoid trouble within the
family and, sharing his/her parents' values, he/she looks for a person of the
appropriate social level who is personally attractive to him/her. A "good

match" was made by Henrietta, the daughter of a wealthy building contractor who married the son of a respected family. The community evaluation of this match was that the boy married for love and the beauty of the girl, as well as for her father's money (although women retain their money and property in their own names after marriage, the husband can have access to it), whereas the girl married for the increased prestige resulting from the association with a distinguished local family. Her family's wealth and her own beauty compensated for her family's inferior social position, and she "married well."

However, whereas the two generations share similar values and beliefs regarding the principles of mate selection, there is frequently great conflict over the actual choice. This conflict arises from the fact that the prestige system permits incongruity between self-estimation and community estimation. That is, while an individual's prestige stratum is fixed by his occupation, his position within that stratum is altered by the elements of "blood," style and spirituality, and his understanding of his own position in the prestige stratum may not coincide with the community's assessment of his position. Thus, parents may see themselves as social superiors to the family (which the community regards as their equals) their child is courting and object to the match. As a consequence, when Johnny McKeague, a 40-year-old teacher, despaired of convincing his mother of the worthiness of his fiancée, he was secretly married without his mother's knowledge in Drumkil. "You could've heard his bloody mother screaming three miles away when she heard her wee boy got married." Again, Rachel, the daughter of an Aughnaboy factory owner, made a "poor match" when, in spite of the extreme disapproval of her parents, she eloped with the labourer she had been courting for fifteen years. Kept single by her prestige-conscious parents, Rachel found herself approaching the menopause without her parents' approval of her lover or the prospect of another being interested in her, and so she eloped with her labourer. Aughnaboy, while applauding her courage and initiative, felt it a poor match, a "come-down" for the family, and a source of embarrassment to all of them in years to come.

Yet most parents are forced to conceal and gloss over their objections to a child's mate by the time marriage is seriously broached, for they are unwilling to risk the humiliation of quarrels and disputes becoming public knowledge, or risk splitting the family; and they are rarely called upon to do so, for most young people pick their mates with an eye to their parents' sensibilities – except in those relatively few "love matches" where the feelings of kin and community must be affronted in order to please the young couple.

The combination of these prohibitions and preferences narrow the category of potential mates available to an individual in any class stratum.

Of those who are available, he/she will eventually choose one whom he/she will "settle down to court" and, perhaps, eventually marry. During the course of a young man's social adolescence, he will court many girls and eventually, if his parents do not strongly disapprove, he will select one over the others on the basis of their mutual compatibility for long-term courtship. Their relationship becomes a permanent one, recognized by themselves, their families, and their communities. They spend many evenings together at dances, films, by the fire with their families, and in their cars on deserted beaches. If sexual intercourse is discouraged by the girl, the boy's persistent demands usually lead in this direction, and the widespread availability and use of contraception minimize the incidence of unwanted pregnancies. Their relationship continues in this fashion, socially and sexually satisfactory to most. If and when the situation so dictates, they marry.

FACTORS PRECIPITATING MARRIAGE

The factors precipitating marriage have been the subject of much comment and debate among students of Irish society. The Irish marry less and at a later age than any other nation for which statistics are available; in 1945–46, the Eire farmer remained single (on the average) until he was thirty-eight, and of farmers between sixty-five and seventy-four, one in four was still a bachelor (Connell, 1962). According to Connell (1968), this "apparent aversion to marriage" which characterizes Irish peasant society was influenced by the Great Famine of the 1840s and the consequent struggle for land. For Connell (1962), Irish peasant marriage was more of an economic contract than a biological institution; ... "it was part of the mechanism that perpetuated the rural economy," and marriage "was likely to be contemplated, not when a man needed a wife, but when the land needed a woman." Economic factors shaped these marriage patterns; fear of recreating the pre-famine situation of constant fragmentation of land created a reality in which only one son and one daughter could be married out of the house. The son married when his father passed over the farm to him, and the daughter married when her father had the necessary dowry.

They married because a "boy," not needing a wife until his mother could no more milk the cows, was not entitled to one until his father, at last, made over the land ... They married little because though the normal family was large, only one of its boys and one of its girls married like their parents into peasant society: for the others (save in emigration) there was small chance of wife or husband (Connell, 1968).

Lending support to this anti-marriage trend, continues Connell, was the anti-sexuality of Irish Catholicism, in which the "ill-educated peasant priests of Maynooth" continually if unwittingly crossed "the shadowy line dividing godly chastity from sinful renunciation of marriage." "All too readily the over-zealous confessor instilled in simple penitents not only a caution of marriage, but their reputed 'complete and awful chastity.'" In this manner, the dominant Irish religion transmitted a sexual and moral code which gave divine sanction to the "patriarchal and material" needs and ambitions of the Irish peasantry.

Symes (1972) has commented that Arensberg and Kimball see marriage and inheritance as "virtually inseparable events [which] occur within, but only just within the parents' life-time: 'when the old couple relinquish the farm, they enter the age grade of the dying'" (Connell, 1962). Irish peasant marriage was linked with the transfer of land and in County Clare, marriage involved a drastic change in the family group, uniting the "transfer of economic control, land ownership, reformation of family ties, advance in family and community status, and entrance into adult procreative sex life" (Arensberg and Kimball, 1940:107). From the point of view of the father, marriage of his son "means the abandonment of the ownership he has long enjoyed; from the point of view of the old woman, it means she is no longer the 'woman of the house'" (op. cit.:123). Such an institution is not to be lightly entered into, nor is it likely to be contracted for everyone. The small farm in County Clare can provide marriages for only one son and one daughter, and the marriages which can be arranged must be delayed until the father is ready and willing to transfer ownership of his farm to his son and to provide a dowry for his daughter.

In Aughnaboy too, marriages tend to be later than elsewhere in the British Isles, with the average age for men (in a sampled thirty-eight marriages) being twenty-eight. Yet the constraints which shape this pattern are rather different from those described for the rest of Ireland. The inhabitants of Aughnaboy are not Roman Catholics, and therefore not subject to a religion which sanctifies chastity. Nor are they peasant farmers who must wait for marriage until the "land needs a woman," since only 10 percent of the villagers are farmers. Nor must they wait for years to be able to afford marriage, as Aughnaboy is a prosperous community, and a labourer or a fisherman makes from £15 to £30 a week from the day he finishes his apprenticeship. Yet they too tend to marry late, or even not at all.

The explanation for this lies in the structure of power relations within the family. The domestic group formed by the nuclear family or unmarried siblings is the ultimate source of affection in Aughnaboy; it is around the family hearth that the most intimate confidences can be exchanged, the most unfettered display of emotional love be permitted. Within the security and intimacy of the home, the youngest child is passed from father to mother to brother to be fondled, hugged, and indulged. Here men and women are able to drop the air of caution and restraint which govern their relations with "strangers": it is this atmosphere which welds the family together in its intense affect, its solidarity, and in its opposition to the outside world.

The strength of these bonds within the family prompted Fox (1965) to remark that, in Ireland, to marry is to "betray one's family." To marry is to suggest to the family that they are incapable of providing for one's emotional needs, that there is another person with whom one would rather sit at another hearth. The jealousy and pain this arouses is well recognized in the literature, and Connell himself (1962) has commented on how the mother typically "fancies herself the rightful object of her boy's affection" and bitterly resents the image of a daughter-in-law – "a woman, brought in to help with the housework, but bold enough to steal her son's affection." But mothers extend these sympathies not only to their sons, but also to daughters who contemplate marriage.

Parents are the ultimate source of power within the family and they expect to have active control of their children's affairs throughout their lives. To maintain their central position, the parents have at their disposal the twin sanctions of withdrawal of affect (with all its attendant public humiliation) and withdrawal of familial occupational aid (with its serious economic repercussions). In these ways, then, parents have sufficient power to postpone their children's marriage over an extended period. Only when "circumstances" change do they consider relenting, and allow the child to leave his or her natal home.

The expressed folk model for this change in circumstances which precipitates marriage for the majority of the villagers is in terms of the need for role replacement at the death of one of the courting couple's parents. A girl who has lost her father will talk about the need for a man in the house; if her mother has died, she will stress that it is now time for her to fulfill the moral imperative of a family – the continuous succession of mother and children. Similarly, a boy who has lost his mother will talk about the household's new need for a woman; if his father has died, it is now appropriate for him to "become a man" and start his own family.

However, these public explanations are but social strategies, rationalizations for the important shifts in the family's power structure which now make marriage possible. In fact, the death of one parent erodes the power of the surviving parent. A widow does not have the means to obtain the occupational aid which her husband had proffered her son; and she may now need a new breadwinner in the house both for herself and her daughter. A widower requires a woman to do his housework, and a son's wife is a suitable source for these services: so too, a husband for his daughter is a new source of income.

With one parent dead then, the arguments against marriage lose their strength, and the sanctions to oppose the marriage weaken. What occurs is that the surviving parent is placed in a position where it is less to his/her disadvantage for the child to marry. At the same time, the child is now in a stronger position to demand the right to marry. There is no automatic acquiescence in this from the surviving parent. But these new pressures make it more likely that the parent will be forced to relent in the face of the youth's strengthened demands.

The actual patterns of marriage accord closely with the above formulation. Of 38 marriages, 82 percent did not take place until one of the courting partner's parents had died, deserted the family, or had been permanently committed to a mental institution – that is, suffered actual or social death. It could perhaps be argued that this is inevitable in an area where people marry relatively late, but in 50 percent of these cases, the marriage occurred within five years of the death of the parent.

Once a youth's parent has died, he begins to look for a mate or, if he is already courting, he begins to pressure her to marry. The person he or she is courting may try to postpone the match until the need for marriage is mutual, but the party initially demanding marriage can threaten to sever the relationship if the union does not take place in the near future. The villagers themselves are well aware of local men whose mothers were dead and whose girlfriends were unwilling to marry; these men then "upped and married" other girls. The threat of this is often effective, for when an individual has invested five, ten, or twenty years in courting one person, the threat of severing the relationship can be a powerful one. Similarly, the party urging marriage may force the match by allowing pregnancy to occur: the girl may allow intercourse, if it was not already being practised, and simultaneously discourage or make inconvenient the use of contraceptives; the boy may neglect to use his contraceptives. Such measures, however, are usually unnecessary – and undesirable, for they bring with them the shame of pre-marital pregnancy and the consequent loss of prestige.

For the majority of the population whose marriages are subject to these forces, the relationship of "courting" continues for extended periods. The couples rationalize the situation in terms of the undesirability of "jumping" into marriage. "There's no need to rush things"; "we're too young to marry yet." These arrangements produce no great conflict for those whose parents die at a reasonable age; but those whose parents continue to live past their "allotted time" are often deprived of marriage. In 1969, Minnie had been courting her man for thirty-seven years; still living with her parents who were in their eighties, she publicly explained her situation as one in which there was "no call for getting married yet"; nor could her man admit to being inconvenienced as his parents were also "fit and healthy."

Marriages that follow from the death of a parent account for the majority of marriages; however, there are two additional factors which we may say actually precipitate marriage in Aughnaboy. Here I refer to quarrels between kin, and the principle of prestige maximization. Regarding the former, quarrels with kin often precipitate marriage – when they do not precipitate emigration (or both). If an individual's kinsmen are cut off as a source of support and affect, he/she will often turn to his/her spouse for these needs. In this manner, Sam Philpott lived with his bachelor brother Bob until they "fell out" and Sam was "thrown out" of Bob's house. Sam was then "forced to marry" the girl he had courted for twenty-two years simply in order to "have a place to sleep"; and she was willing because she lived alone with her widowed mother, and both needed a man in the house.

Prestige maximization is significant in those cases where a girl has the opportunity of marrying a boy of greater wealth and prestige – too tempting a prize to be allowed to slip through her fingers.

RITUAL

The wedding, itself, the ritual cementing of the union between man and wife and between their respective kin, is usually announced from six months to a year in advance. Arrangements are made for furniture and a home to house the couple, and church and hotel are booked. The wedding normally involves from thirty to one hundred guests, depending on the wealth of the bride's parents who must pay for the ceremony and the reception following it.

Custom dictates who should be invited to the wedding, and customary procedure is subject only to the limitations of family disputes and neces-sary economies. The bride and groom each invite their siblings and their spouses, their parents, grandparents, and two representatives from each household of their parents' siblings (that is, either uncles and aunts or their children). In addition, if the bride's parents are wealthy enough, a few "mates" of the bride and groom and their parents are occasionally invited. The ideal pattern is not possible for everyone because of the expense, and people are not expected to go deeply into debt for a wedding; consequently, the poorer the bride's parents, the more the guest list is restricted to the nuclear families of the bride and groom. Great efforts, however, are made to approach the ideal. Conversely, any attempts to expand the guest list are met with considerable resistance. In one case, when the bride attempted to invite more than two representatives from each of the parents' siblings' households – *all* her full cousins, the cousins refused to attend on the grounds that it was inappropriate and setting an expensive precedent which they would then be expected to follow.

The actual wedding is performed in the bride's church, her last contact with the church if her husband is from outside Aughnaboy (they will now attend his so long as it is within Perrin), and her last contact with her denomination if her husband is a member of another. The women of the bride's community gather outside the church to observe and comment on the appearance of the bride and the wedding procession. Inside the church, the bride's kin and friends sit on the left side of the church, and the groom's kin and friends sit on the right, expressing in spatial form the solidarity and separateness of the kindreds. During the ceremony, the bride walks down the left aisle of the church, down "her side" to meet her father who gives her away during the short and simple Protestant ritual. Then, with her husband, she walks up the right aisle, up "his side" of the church. The invited guests then travel to the hotel for the reception and banquet, where to symbolize the new alliance of the two kindreds, the parties of bride and groom are carefully mixed at each table to give emphasis to the bonds and obligations which are now to unite them all.

MORAL OBLIGATIONS TO AFFINES

It is not without significance that affines are referred to as "connexions," the same term that is occasionally used to refer to "far out" cognates – those with whom the exact relationship is forgotten, the quality and content of the relationship unspecified, and the strength of the obligations minimal. The classificatory situation is similar to Campbell's Sarakatsani, where relationships can be "claimed not only with the elementary family of origin of a person's spouse, or the elementary family of origin of the wife or husband of any member in a person's kindred, but also with the entire kindred of the marriage partner" (1964:138). Any of these individuals can be claimed as "friends by marriage," and favours can be demanded of them on the basis of this relationship.

But the conceptualization and honouring of obligations is more complex than this, for the matter of affinal obligations is subject to class-generated dissensus. Here the important distinction is between marriages of unequals and marriages of equals. In marriages of class unequals – there develops a very different affinal ideology than that found in the marriages of equals. Among the former, for example, a man's wife's family may possess greater authority, wealth, or prestige, and it is to the man's advantage to maximize his interest in his affines and to minimize the significance of his own cognates. Among these people, affines assume great significance; a subtle shift of loyalties and identification from cognates to affines takes place. Geordie, whose father was a breadserver in County Antrim, married an Aughnaboy woman whose personal attributes rendered her unlikely for marriage but whose family had considerable wealth and prestige. He moved into his wife's home after marriage, and began the process of identifying himself with his affines. To increase his identification with his affines and to neglect his association with his own lower-prestige cognates was to enhance his own position in Aughnaboy. In describing the situation, Geordie remarked: "when a man is married, it's the wife's people that come first; the husband's people are put in the background. The wife says we're going to my mother and he just tags along."

Similarly, it is expected that affines will be "close" to an individual; that men should be ready to help their affines in times of emergency; and that, after marriage, the individual is seen slowly being absorbed as one with his affines. These newly forged bonds carry with them moral obligations of a similar order to those reserved for cognates by the remainder of the village. "They wouldn't put you out of a job to put one of their own (kin) in." For these men the shift of loyalty and identification from cognates to affines is profound.

However, for the majority of the villagers whose marriages take place largely between those of roughly equal class strata, the speeches at the wedding ceremonies and the headlines in the local newspapers announcing a marriage with the words "Perrin Families United" are regarded as a public fiction. Marriage is not so much an act of alliance and union as it is an institution which forces its members to participate in uneasy and uncertain relations with a group of persons towards whom one is not bound by the loyalties and trust implicit in the ties between blood kin. In general, affines "aren't friends at all," and villagers pretend an attitude of affection and concern as best they can. They occasionally support their affines in order to "keep the peace" in the house; "but there really isn't any tie at all." Yet the villagers recognize that the children of one's close affines are one's blood kin, for a son's marriage with a "stranger" produces a grandchild, and a brother's marriage with a "stranger" produces a nephew or niece. The ties with affines and the obligations to them are built upon this knowledge; while there is no change in their exclusive solidarity and identity with their own cognates, individuals are forced to establish and maintain cordial relations with their affines, and to acquiesce in cooperation and in the dispensation of favours when conditions so dictate.

Men perform favours for an affine not because they are "under an obligement" to that person, but because of the affine's relationship to his own cognate or spouse. An individual will rarely volunteer to help an affine; if and when he does help, he does so at his wife's request to satisfy her and to avoid the implication that he is deprecating her worth by ignoring or refusing to help her kinsmen. An instance of this kind of claim occurred when McDonagh's mate, Bristol, returned from America bankrupt after a spending spree, and needed to be placed on the dole quickly. The form-filling and the regulations governing this normally involve the expenditure of considerable time and effort, yet Bristol needed the money immediately. McDonagh went to see his brother's wife's father, an official in the employment bureau. McDonagh first reminded his brother's father-in-law that he (McDonagh) would soon be repairing the latter's door, and then asked him to expedite Bristol's request. Bristol was on the dole the following day.

The critical affinal relation for most class strata is with a man's spouse's family and kindred. So long as he maintains "decent" relations with them, he is not driving a wedge between himself and his wife, and he is assuring himself and his children of adequate support in times of crisis. In the final analysis, individuals are more or less coerced – by the needs of their children, their spouse and themselves – into assuming or pretending to assume an attitude of affection, loyalty, and trust towards their affines. The pressure for the maintenance of this charade is greatest with his wife's kin; he cannot avoid those with whom he may be forced to spend endless evenings by the fireside and who may be continually in and out of his own house. Although they are enjoined to joke and tease and laugh with their affines as if they were kinsmen, it is in fact the red face, the fixed smile, the false guffaw and the awkward shuffle which are mannerisms characteristic of these meetings between affines. However, for most strata, little more than a respectful attitude is necessary with the whole range of a man's spouse's kin; major favours such as lending money or finding a berth on a trawler occur only with his wife's siblings and parents and these, in fact, are the parameters of normal cooperation between affines.

Nevertheless, relations between affines, especially in these equal marriages, are a constant source of tension, and affinity provokes more disputes than any other social category in Aughnaboy. As I have mentioned elsewhere (Leyton, 1966), the social bonds between affines contain the greatest potential and actual conflict. They are characterized by an absence of affective relations and a high degree of potential competition. While a marriage between equals forges few bonds, it creates a situation of great competition for affection and control between ego's spouse and ego's natal family. The natal family tends to see the in-marrying spouse as an individual who offers little or nothing of value, and only threatens the substance and solidarity of their relationships; indeed, 49 percent of all disputes recorded in the village took place between affines.

In sum then, I have examined some aspects of marriage in Aughnaboy, notably the factors influencing mate selection and those precipitating marriage, as well as the differential conceptions of obligation and identity which are associated with equal and unequal marriages.

Part III: Kinship and Economy

Inheritance

7

I have reserved this and the following chapter for a more detailed discussion of the institutions of inheritance and economy in which the intrusion of kinship is most apparent. In Aughnaboy, the transmission of goods between the generations occurs exclusively among kinsmen; it is a realm in which class-generated dissensus in kinship ideology and behaviour is clearly delineated.

No single pattern exists for inheritance in Ireland. In County Clare (Arensberg and Kimball, 1940), inheritance is linked with marriage, with the transfer of economic control during the life of the parents, and with the reformation of family ties as the new couple moves into the house and slowly establishes control of the household and farm. Here, only one son can be provided for on the farm – and one daughter married into another farm – and the remaining children "must travel." Contrasting markedly with this pattern is the complex "clan" system described by Fox (1966) for Tory Island, where inheritance of land "is bilateral in the sense that both men and women can own and transmit land, and that all a person's children, regardless of sex, have a *claim* on the land." Aughnaboy's inheritance system differs from both of these in important ways; essentially, a consensus ideology defines the nature and scope of obligation between a person and his various kinsmen, whereas class interests dictate dissensual ideologies regarding the actual patterns of transmission.

CONSENSUS

There are a number of important values and beliefs which are shared by all the villagers. One is simply that no property of any kind should ever be passed beyond the range of the kindred. Although no exceptions to this rule were recorded in Aughnaboy, the village is full of tales of such practices which are reputed to have occurred in neighbouring villages and townlands. For example, a son stayed at home, remaining unmarried and working on his widowed father's farm; on the father's death, the farm did not pass to the son who so richly deserved it, but to a village trollop who had "entertained him" during his dotage. Such stories, however, are clearly sanctions in the form of examples of moral depravity, or expressions of nightmarish anxiety, rather than accurate descriptions of empirical fact; for no specific and named examples of such occurrences could ever be given by the villagers, and no property has ever passed to non-kin (other than spouses).

Another shared value stems from the central position of the family. As I have remarked throughout this monograph, a man's supreme obligations are to his children throughout his life. His last act in life (the repercussions of which do not make themselves felt until after his death) is to pass what property he has to his children or, lacking children, to members of his kindred. As it is his last act, it is also the discharge of his final obligation; and accordingly, he must ensure that his property is passed with justice to the person or persons who, in Aughnaboy's ideology, are ''most entitled'' to it and who deserve it the most. As such, when he is deciding who shall inherit his worldly goods, he must consider providing as many of his children as possible with as many material goods as he can, and as many of his sons as possible with the resources for their occupations: funds for the continuation of their education, or items of fixed capital such as trawlers, businesses, or farms. Additionally, he must ensure that his goods are so divided that they reflect the measure and quality of his love and respect for the various members of his family, as inheritance is the mechanism for the final reward of those who have done the most to earn his affection and trust. Thus, from the children's point of view, inheritance is not only a source of financial or material gain, but it is also a source of psychic gain as it is a public statement of love and esteem. Again, a man is obliged to ensure the well-being of his wife if she is widowed and to provide for unmarried daughters.

These basic obligations are reinforced by the state. Government legislation demands that a man be responsible for maintaining his wife until she remarries, his daughter until she marries, his son until he reaches the age of twenty-one, and his disabled child until he is cured. The main effect of this and other legislation is to reinforce Aughnaboy custom.

There are a number of additional shared ideals and preferences which influence the inheritance patterns. An important one, and one which contrasts markedly with County Clare's practice of announcing the inheritance well before the death of the owner, is what can be called the Lear Principle: the notion that no property should be transferred until the death of the owner. The belief here is that money and property tie the children to their parents, and to transfer these before one's death – or even to announce who will receive them – is to risk losing not only the control but also the affection and attention of one's children. It is not just the actual transfer of goods that is delayed but the decision itself is often not made, and rarely announced before the owner finds himself on his death bed. Consequently, it is often necessary for relatives to compete with each other for the esteem of the owner until the moment of his death. The only exceptions to this principle occur when it is necessary for the individual to dispose of his property in order to obtain the welfare benefits of National Assistance. Thus, even when actual operational control of a farm or business has passed to a son, the retired father normally retains legal control of the enterprise – and social control of his son – unless his income is sufficiently low to necessitate formal transmission in order to obtain pensions and assistance.

An additional preference is that inheritance normally should go to the generation immediately below the owner of the property. Thus a man should leave his property to his children or, if he has no children, to his nephews and nieces rather than to his brothers and sisters. He usually does so, for his brothers and sisters are regarded as fully grown and well-established in their own right and correspondingly less likely to need the property than their children who may be "just starting off."

The final set of general ideals and preferences shared by the whole community regards the priorities assigned to different types of kin. Essentially, the villagers use two sets of oppositions to determine the relative strength of their obligations to a given kinsman: those of kinship category (cognate/affine, patrinominal kin/all others) and those of genealogical distance (family/kindred, full cousin/half cousin). This method of reckoning obligation is of considerable importance to a man when he is deciding which way his estate shall be willed, and it is worth examining these in greater detail. At the broadest level is the priority of cognates over all affines. This is an inflexible value which, nevertheless, gives rise to much anxiety in Aughnaboy, for the countryside is filled with stories – once again generally unsubstantiated – of men who gave their property without condition to their wives, who in turn remarried and "gave it to a stranger." Accordingly then, when there is a surviving spouse, the property normally is passed directly to the children, with the proviso that the spouse be cared for "for her time"; or it may be passed to the spouse with the provision that upon her death or remarriage, the property reverts to the owner's cognates. When McKeague, a chronically unemployed labourer from Drumkil, married Annie, he came to live with her in her house in Aughnaboy; when Annie died she left her house to her son Henry, with the proviso that her husband be allowed to remain in the house until he died or remarried. Two years later, when McKeague remarried, he left the house.

An additional preference relevant here concerns the distinctions made on the basis of age and sex of siblings. There is a tendency to give rather more to sons than to daughters; this preference is normally rationalized in terms of statements that daughters will have husbands to provide for them whereas sons must strike out on their own.

In sum, consensus ideology exists regarding the priority of kin over "strangers," of cognates over affines, of family over kindred, and of sons over daughters. But dissensus reigns in other matters.

DISSENSUS

It is important first to distinguish what I have referred to elsewhere as "spheres of inheritance" (Leyton, 1970a), or those different forms of value (major items of capital, houses, and money) which are transmitted according to different principles. The spheres can be conceptualized as occupying different positions in a continuum in which money is at one end and major items of capital are at the other, with houses occupying an intermediate position. *Money* is transmitted bilaterally, flows bisexually to and from both sexes, and is more likely to flow to members of the wider kindred than within the family (only 42 percent of recorded transmissions were within the family). Major items of *capital* flow patrilaterally and unisexually through males, and remain largely within the family (only 18 percent of the transmissions went to extra-familial kin). The movement of *houses* falls halfway between the patrilateral/bilateral, unisexual/bisexual and family/kindred extremes of the continuum (73 percent of houses were transmitted within the family). Tables 4 and 5 summarize the characteristic transmission of the three forms of value.

Inheritance of Money: Masses' Model
Among the masses, money (the amounts recorded in the inheritances ranged from £100 to £100,000, the average being under £2,000) is seen as a reward for services performed and as a means of acknowledging the favourite(s) among one's family and kindred: "money usually goes to whoever treated them the best." At the same time, however, no child wishes to think that his parents loved him less than another, and there is likely to be considerable offence taken if the money is not shared with a semblance of rough equality between all children. Thus the individual drawing up his will must exercise the greatest delicacy in the distribution of his money, since no man wishes to leave jealousy and resentment in his wake.

Money is not rigidly attached to males or to the name, and if a man or woman is childless, he/she does not feel the same need to transmit it to, for example, a brother's son, but is free to give it to any favoured member of his kindred. In addition, money is readily divisible, unlike fixed capital or houses. This is the normal situation, and as can be seen in Table 5, money is even more likely to come from kinsmen other than parents and from kindred rather than family – a characteristic which is displayed by no other form of value. Table 5 summarizes the patterns of actual transmissions and shows that women are even more likely than men to receive money (if a son gets a farm, a daughter will get some of the money).

The cases below illustrate the general pattern of transmission of money among the masses. Robbie Hale, a widowed farmer with three sons and one daughter, willed £2,000 as compensation to his eldest son who had been most entitled to the farm but who had turned it down and emigrated to Australia, £500 to the youngest son who worked in a Belfast factory, no money to the middle son who had inherited the farm and house in the eldest son's place, £300 to his daughter who was married to a policeman, and £100 to his sister's daughter who, while a resident for twenty-five years in the United States, spent every summer with Robbie in Aughnaboy. In a second case, Bertie Foster left a total of £2,000 which was willed equally to his three daughters and two sons. A third case involves the division of Cissy Jones' estate of £8,000. Cissy was survived by her only daughter, middle-aged and married, and her daughter's two children. Cissy has "never got on that well" with her own daughter who had "married badly," but she "worshipped" her grandchildren. She divided her money equally between them, leaving nothing to her daughter.

Inheritance of Money: Elites' Model

Among the elites, however, where the amount of money involved is some-times so large that it can provide a living for its owner, money is seen as quite a separate ideology: the large sum virtually becomes (is thought of as) an item of fixed capital. Hence, it is distributed according to the more formal "name" and kin category which governs the sphere of fixed capital. This elite conception is illustrated in the case of Gordie McOnachie. A bachelor, McOnachie emigrated to South Africa in the early 1920s and accumulated a "fortune" of approximately £100,000 in his business opera-tions. He never returned to Aughnaboy although he continued to write to members of his family. When he died, he was survived by one brother's daughter, four half-siblings by his father's second marriage, and six half-siblings by his mother's first marriage. McOnachie willed his money as follows: the £100,000 was divided into six shares, one full share going to

TABLE 4

Transmission of Three Forms of Value by Kinship Category

	Major Capital	Houses	Money
Within Family	57	72	20
Between Kindred	12	19	24
Between Affines	0	7	4
Between Non-Kin	0	0	0
Totals	69	98	48

TABLE 5

Inheritance[1] of Three Forms of Value by Kin Type, and Sex of Recipient

	House	Money	Fixed Capital	Totals
From parents	68 (23)	17 (9)	55 (5)	140
From siblings	4 (2)	3 (3)	2 (1)	9
From paternal grandparents	4 (1)	0 (0)	1 (0)	5
From maternal grandparents	2 (0)	4 (0)	1 (0)	7
From father's brothers	7 (1)	2 (0)	5 (0)	14
From all other "uncles" and "aunts"	5 (4)	11 (7)	1 (0)	17
From father's father's brothers	0 (0)	3 (3)	1 (0)	4
From all other "great-uncles" and "great-aunts"	1 (0)	4 (2)	3 (1)	8
From husband	7 (7)	4 (4)	0 (0)	11
From non-kin	0 (0)	0 (0)	0 (0)	0
Totals	98 (38)	48 (28)	69 (7)	215

N.B. the first number denotes the total number of recipients; the second number, in brackets, denotes the number of female recipients.

1 By inheritance, I refer to the transmission of each piece of property, house, or money; thus, when a man leaves his trawler to his son, his house to his daughter, and divides his money between his wife, son, and daughter, I am talking about five inheritances: the passage of one major item of capital, one house, and three portions of money. The 215 inheritances discussed here involve members of 105 different households.

each of his father's second wife's four children, one full share going to his dead brother's daughter, one-half share to one of the sons of his mother's first marriage who had corresponded faithfully with McOnachie over the years, and one-half share to this same half-brother's spinster daughter.

Inheritance of Major Capital: Elites' Model

The different flow patterns revealed by the different forms of property in Tables 4 and 5 are largely a consequence of the different interests of the two wealth strata: those who own capital and those who do not. Those elites who own major capital such as farms, businesses, and trawlers, from which their owners derive their primary source of income, have an inheritance ideology which emphasizes the family, the name, eldest sons, and males. A man's ultimate obligations are to his family, and it is "only natural" that he should leave his capital to them. If he has no sons, "the mother's side drops out; a McPherson wants to leave it to a McPherson, holding it in the one name.'' The substance and renown of a family is inextricably tied to its property (not just to its farms), and for the property to pass out of the name diminishes the prestige and worth of the family.

These two variables of family and name are balanced together, with priority going to the family when a decision must be made: thus if a man has no sons, the emphasis on the family will force him to give it to his daughters; but if he has no children, he will pass his property to male members of his kindred who bear the same name.

The unisexual and male/male emphasis of those who own major capital is a function of the idea that occupational and economic affairs belong to men, and that sons must be provided for before daughters, as daughters will marry men with other names who will be responsible for providing for them. McLintock, a ''big farmer'' with over one hundred acres, had one son and one daughter. His son married and went into the Civil Service paying little attention to McLintock. His daughter, on the other hand, married a relatively poor fisherman and ''could have used the farm.'' But the farm went to McLintock's son: ''I want it kept in the name.''

Finally, owners of major capital believe that the eldest son is ''most entitled'' to inherit; if he is not interested in inheriting the property (many sons despise farming and ''want no part of it''), then he must be ''compensated'' for the passage of ''his'' farm to a younger brother.

Inheritance of Major Capital: Masses' Model

Those who do not own major capital, however, are not as tied to the principles of ''the name'' and the preference for eldest sons. They believe that major items of property should rightfully go to ''whichever son was the best to the homestead, was the best to the father, and worked the hardest.'' Since these men do not, however, own such capital, their beliefs are not of direct importance to the actual transmissions; but indirectly they are, for their opinions are listened to by younger sons of property owners, and the ambiguity generated by these contrary class views creates what conflict there is over inheritance. A relevant illustration here concerns the two Pendennis brothers who did not speak to each other for twenty years after their father's shop went to the eldest son who had ''been working in England.'' The younger son, tainted by the beliefs of his property-less friends, felt that the shop was rightfully his because he had stayed behind and helped his father in the shop; the elder brother felt it rightfully belonged to him because he was the eldest son, and the ''eldest son is the most entitled.''

In general, however, whereas owners of major capital are more likely to stress patrilaterality and primogeniture, and non-owners more likely to stress 'deserts,' there are no rigid prescriptions, but rather much ambiguity. This ambiguity is extended to nephews when there are no children, and to full cousins when there are neither nephews nor children: consequently, villagers of the appropriate category of prospective heirs must go to considerable lengths to prove that they are the most deserving of that kin category. "Both would be making strenuous efforts to get the farm, there'd be no scruples, there'd be a battle to get in with him, one of the family would be sitting up nights to get it from the other." Indeed, when a propertied man reaches his twilight years, he is the beneficiary of much attention and concern from the category of kin from which his choice will be made. He will also encourage the ambiguity, for if his choice were known, he would lose the attention of his kin. Thus, he will hold off making his will to the last moment – not wishing to sacrifice his comforts prematurely – and depend on the "fast cars" of local lawyers at the final call.

As I have suggested, the owners of major capital are not bound to any rigid prescriptions; unisexual inheritance, "the name," and eldest son are only preferences and expectations which can be altered when circumstances dictate. In fact, five of the twelve recorded inheritances of major capital went to members of the kindred who did not bear the same name. An illustration of this flexibility, of the kinds of circumstances which can affect preferences is the following: Jack McCulla was a bachelor who lived in the back of his hardware shop. He had two nephews, Ned McCulla, his brother's son, and Hugh Leach, his sister's son. Normally, the preference for keeping property in the name might automatically cause the shop and house to be passed to Ned. But Ned was a prosperous builder while Hugh was unemployed "through no fault of his own." Recognizing the greater need of his sister's son, Jack willed the shop and attached house to Hugh. Hugh kept the shop and maintained it as an adequate source of income. When he died after a short illness in 1969, his children were all in their twenties and unmarried. The house was willed to his spinster daughter, who was most in need of a place to live, for she had no one to care for her if the boys married; and the shop was willed jointly to all three children.

In general, however, the elite's model prevails in the transmission of major capital items. The fundamental obligation is that capital must be kept in the family or, failing that, within the name. And this must be balanced against the distance of genealogical relationship, for a man is "closer" to his sister's son than he is to his father's brother's son. Thus, the order of preference tends to be son, daughter, brother's son, sister's son, patrilateral parallel full cousin, all other full cousins; this is borne out in the actual transmissions, the vast majority of which occurs between father and son, father and daughter, and father's brother and brother's son.

The cases below illustrate the normal application of these principles. Abraham MacAlinden set up a business in the stone trade in the mid-nineteenth century, quarrying, cutting, and polishing local granite. Abraham had three sons: his eldest son Isaac inherited the stone business and the house, the largest piece of property owned by Abraham; the second son was given a small farm; and the third son inherited a small grocery shop which Abraham also owned. In the next generation, the house and stone business passed from Abraham's oldest son Isaac to Isaac's only son Russell. In addition, Isaac's two brothers, who had remained childless, passed the grocery shop and the farm to Russell on their deaths. Although actual control of the stone yard – which gives its owner an annual income in excess of £5,000 – was in Russell's hands well before his father's death, no legal provisions for this passage were made until shortly before his father's death.

The second case involves the inheritance of a 55-acre farm with a present-day market value of approximately £15,000. Willy McAnn, whose father was a stone-cutter, was interested in farming. Willy's father's brother, James, who was childless and a farmer, took Willy into his home as an adolescent and raised him, and Willy accordingly inherited James's farm. At Willy's death, the farm passed to his second son Geordie, who had stayed at home and not married, while Willy's other two sons were provided with smaller farms elsewhere in the district.

A third case involves the transfer of Charlie Fairleigh's two farms with a market value of approximately £24,000. Charlie was survived by two sons and four daughters; three of the daughters had married, and the fourth had remained unmarried and stayed at home to "take care" of Charlie. Charlie left his largest farm, with a market value of about £16,000, to his eldest son (his youngest was a builder with "no interest" in farming), and the smaller farm to his spinster daughter. The remaining son and three daughters were each given a token sum of £130, an act which infuriated them and, indeed, left the family in a state of extreme tension. Nevertheless, the community regarded the inheritance as a just one, if unnecessarily unkind to the remaining children.

Inheritance of Houses

Just as different class interests generate dissensus in the masses' and elites' ideology regarding the inheritance of major capital, the inheritance of houses is similarly effected. But houses are mid-point in the continuum between capital and money; a few houses are transmitted according to the principle of the name, but more are transmitted according to "deserts" and "need." Excepting those who own major capital, it is believed that a house should go to whoever deserves it the most or needs it the most.

Those elites who own major capital often also own a house which is (literally) attached to or traditionally associated with the enterprise. Whether it is the house on the farm or the home beside the shop or stone yard, the house bears the name of the family, and is normally of higher quality and greater cost than available alternatives. As such, the "home place" is part of the capital estate, and must pass according to the preferences which condition the movement of capital.

For the masses, however, who sometimes own houses, the "home place" does not have such important associations. For them, houses do not have the same significance as major property, and the primary criteria are "deserts" and "need." Indeed, the rivalry for houses in Aughnaboy is muted in comparison to the rivalry for other items, as cheap rented housing is a ready alternative in the village with rents ranging from ten to forty shillings per week. Furthermore, houses are of relatively little financial value, the market value of the workman's cottage (in 1965) ranging from £400 to £1,000. This is not to suggest that the villagers place no value on houses. There is the sentimental value attached to the "home place" where the family was raised. But since alternatives are readily available, villagers rarely feel that houses are worth fighting over and disturbing the delicate balance of family and kindred: "the main thing is to preserve the family friendship."

The above notions are illustrated in the case of Frankie Jordan who died leaving three children and two houses. Rather than offend one of his children by leaving him out of the will, he simply left the two houses jointly to the three children, asking that they settle the division themselves. One of the daughters had recently built her own modern house, and so she "didn't need it"; the only son was already living in one of the father's houses and as the first married, he had claimed it years before. The other daughter "had stayed with them (the parents) and was most entitled to it, so she got it."

Table 5 summarizes the actual behaviour regarding the inheritance of houses which are passed to females as well as to males and to kindred as well as to family. There would be an even greater proportion of houses passed to females were it not for the already mentioned fact that many houses are associated with major items of fixed capital and, as such, are automatically transmitted along with the farm or ship. It is also prefered that the "home place" stay in the name, as long as this does not conflict with the needs of daughters. The large number of females who have inherited houses normally do so by remaining unmarried and staying at home to care for their aging parents, an act which gives them greater entitlement to the house. But the house is normally passed to them "for their time" only, after which the house is most often passed back into the name. Accordingly, when Anna Prentice's widowed father died, she inherited his house because she nursed him until he died, by which time she was in her 60's herself and still unmarried. Anna's brother and sister had both married and emigrated to England, and Anna was the one who needed the house most. A second case involves the transfer of a house and attached farm. Andrew Smith and his two unmarried brothers jointly inherited their house and farm from their father in the 1920s. On Andrew's death in the 1940s, the farm and house passed to Andrew's eldest son Adam, with the proviso that Andrew's spinster daughter have "a place" in the house until she married or died.

Disputes over Inheritance

In spite of the ideological dissensus and ambiguity, serious disputes over inheritance are relatively rare; indeed, they represent less than 5 percent of the total number of disputes recorded in the village. This is partly because rarely is the amount involved considered to be of overriding significance. Most men do not have wealth and property, a labourer's value of earthly goods totalling between £100 and £1,000. When Willy Tague died, having been a pensioner for more than 25 years, he left only his savings book containing £120, old pieces of furniture with almost no market value, and his clothing. When Hugh Wilson, a 47-year-old lorry driver, died, he left his Ford valued at £300, savings of approximately £250, his personal possessions and furniture. These are not estates of sufficient value for the younger and more prosperous generation of Aughnaboy to compete for with vehemence, since quarreling over an inheritance is sullying the memory of the dead and, more importantly, risking the loss of all future support of one's kindred; and to quarrel openly about an inheritance is to expose oneself and one's family to the social disgrace which must accompany familial discord.

This is not to denigrate the importance of inheritance in Aughnaboy, for it is in fact important in the lives of the villagers. But the loss of an inheritance is not an irreparable one, as it might be for example among Campbell's Sarakatsani shepherds who have few alternative sources of income. In Aughnaboy, men can and do become, without debilitating loss of face or income, wage labourers or employees rather than farmers or shopkeepers. Rather, losing an inheritance is to be publicly insulted, for it implies lack of love and esteem, and to be deprived perhaps of added luxuries in one's life. But it is rarely a major economic catastrophe, and no father will see his child so afflicted.

Summary

In Aughnaboy, there are no jural norms or prescriptions which restrict the patterns of inheritance other than the stipulations of the legal system that wife, unmarried daughter, or disabled son be cared for. Nonetheless, inheritance is subject to the dual constraints of class-generated dissensus and different priorities over forms of value.

Although all inheritance occurs exclusively within the orbit of blood kinship, the elites have certain interests in the maintenance of the prestige and wealth of their patronym which make it more important for them to emphasize more formal criteria – especially patronymic inheritance, primogeniture, and "the name." In contrast, among the masses, the three different forms of value – capital, houses, and money – are transmitted according to more flexible criteria. In the sphere of money, reward and "deserts" are given the highest priority; with houses and capital, all the variables of need, deserts, esteem, and kin category are balanced for the final decision.

But for all the men of Aughnaboy, the system of inheritance is open to manipulation and alteration. If the interests of the elites necessitate a decreased flexibility in their decisions, ultimately each person – regardless of his class – must weigh in his own mind his personal love for individuals against his responsibilities to specific kinsmen.

8

In Aughnaboy, a man's primary duties in the economic domain are to provide for the material well-being of his family, and to maintain and, if possible, advance, its wealth and prestige. Hard work is considered virtuous in itself, and the Puritan values of thrift, industriousness, and initiative dominate the villagers' "economic" thinking. The accumulation of money is regarded as a worthy goal for it is both a symbol of initiative and success and a source of prestige and luxury. Money is accumulated through hard work and thrift, and its purposes are thought to be saving and investment as well as expenditure for both subsistence and luxury items.

The highest praise is reserved for the "decent" man who, while avoiding any elaborate conspicuous consumption for prestige purposes, works from dawn to dusk in a life-long struggle to maximize his resources. To fulfill Aughnaboy's ideal, he must temper any success with a cheerful and egalitarian manner, for those whose economic rise is accompanied by "putting on airs" find themselves the subject of great contempt and malicious ridicule. So too must he act with generosity towards his kinsmen and with an absence of "meanness" in his personal affairs, for to be excessively parsimonious is to expose oneself to ridicule. Thus Hearne, who "struck it lucky" prospecting in Canada, and who makes a great display of his gold watch, his cigars, and his expensive cars, cannot walk through Aughnaboy without provoking hoots and sarcastic remarks; and the Murphys, who live in what is regarded as appalling filth and poverty, never spending a penny for a "bit of comfort" or a drink, wearing ragged and lice-ridden clothing, are regarded with even greater distaste, for they have gone entirely beyond the bounds of "decency."

While a man should take some leisure from his work, considerable rationalization is necessary to justify major expenditures for pleasure alone. The merchant who purchased a yacht for purely sporting purposes was subjected to great ridicule, as "he had no call for a boat," and had "wasted" thousands of pounds on an item that had no conceivable economic use. With the exception of pigeon-racing, the only sports that are widely practised are those such as skiff-fishing for mackerel and herring, or rabbit hunting, which can be justified in economic terms: "it's a fine way to make a few pound in an evening." The fishermen who fish inshore for mackerel in the summer evenings after work rarely profit much more than is necessary to pay for the purchase, maintenance, and running of the skiff (although fishing for herring in the short autumn season can bring in £100 per week in good years); yet they are able to justify their sporting activities on the basis of the income received from their catches.

Beyond the general obligation of maintaining with dignity his wife and children, a man's supreme obligations in the economic realm are to provide for the future of his aging parents and his maturing sons. He must assist his parents if and when they are in economic need and ensure that they are able to spend their old age in material and spiritual comfort. If a man allows his parents to be deprived in their old age, or worse, sends them to an Old Folks Home, he has committed unpardonable offenses against his blood and has failed as a man.

Equally strong is his obligation to outfit his sons for their careers. Education is highly valued for its intrinsic merits and for the prestigious occupations it enables one to enter. Only in rare instances is schooling discontinued before the son can bear it no more. When the low status Trent family pulled their protesting son out of school and made him work in the family shop, the community thought the act "incredibly stupid," but "typical of the Trents." Once his sons complete formal schooling, a man is expected to start them in their careers. For the elites, this may take the form of bringing the son on board the family trawler and grooming him to succeed as skipper. Similarly, a shopkeeper or businessman may bring his son into the business and teach him the trade, or he may set him up in another business of his own. For the masses, this obligation normally takes the form of trying to place him in an apprenticeship in one of the higher-paying trades such as brick-laying, plumbing, and carpentry or, failing that, trying to get him a job in the stone yards and quarries, on construction sites, or on board the trawlers. Fathers clearly feel that it is their prerogative to select their sons' first jobs. While sons may feel that with their growing maturity should come a measure of independence in choosing their own jobs according to their own interests and abilities, conflict over this is largely obviated by their relative impotence: "decent" jobs and apprenticeships are most easily obtained through influence and "connexions" to which they have but limited access.

With the passing of time, however, the parents' control tends to diminish with the son's growing maturity. But as I have already suggested, this is less true for the sons of those in the higher wealth and authority strata who own and control major resources such as stone yards, farms, or trawlers. Fathers tend to control their sons' careers for an indefinite period, for the training and employment of their sons is an investment in the future of their own enterprise, and the sons must wait until their fathers grow old and die before they have full control of their own affairs. It is here too that parents' social control over their sons is complete; and sons committed to taking

over their fathers' enterprises can rarely make decisions which are not
congruent with the fathers' wishes. For most men, however, job selection
is a dynamic process, changing over the course of their careers. Parents are
most likely to select their sons' first jobs, but the obligation of the parents
diminishes as the sons mature.

OCCUPATIONAL DISSENSUS

In addition to the generalized obligations which I have described above,
kinship is an important mechanism in the economic affairs of the villager.
Although the nature of this impact varies among the different class strata, it
occurs for all at three points in the economic structure: in obtaining jobs, in
pooling labour and capital, and in providing credit.

In British urban environments, kinship appears to play a relatively minor
role in the occupational sphere. Firth's (1964a) recent London research has
suggested that "direct economic services" are not of major importance;
and Young and Willmott (1957) stress the importance of kinsmen in providing references and news about jobs, but they emphasize that this importance has diminished since the war. In Aughnaboy, however, the critical
generalization is Linton's (1959) remark: "when a man can do better
without relatives than with them, he will tend to ignore the ties of kinship."
In the pages which follow, I shall try to examine the nature and source of
the variation between individuals in both their conceptualization of their
obligations towards kin and in their actual behaviour.

In Aughnaboy, the conflicting interests of the different class strata produce dissensus at virtually every point in the occupational structure insofar
as it relates to the hiring of kin. Indeed, the only value which all classes
share, is the belief in the *undesirability* of working with kin. The "reasons"
given vary from the undesirability of mixing authority relations with kin
("you can't yell at your uncle") to the frustration of working with individuals who have different work habits: "I'd rather work with somebody who
was apprenticed under the same man as I was, for he was taught the same
way of doing things as I was, and you don't have to spend half the day
arguing about the best way to set down a brick." All classes believe that
working with kin is a potential source of difficulty and awkwardness. Yet
most men work, or have worked with kin. But the paradox here is more
apparent than real, for if the masses ardently deny that they "like" working
with kin, they know that it is to their profound advantage to make such
arrangements. For most men, class-generated interests dictate that they
work with kin.

THE MASSES: A KINSHIP IDEOLOGY AND STRATEGY

For those in the lower authority strata who neither own enterprises nor
control hiring (about 79 percent of the male household heads), kinship is of

vital and constant importance, for it is through the network of kinsmen that the masses obtain new jobs when their current jobs have become redundant, and better-paying jobs when conditions allow. This is a continuing need because as I have mentioned above, while Aughnaboy is a prosperous part of Ireland, its wage labour economy is an insecure one. Jobs are scarce (with an unemployment rate of about 20 percent in the '60s) and short-term, individuals being subject to lay-offs at all times. In such an atmosphere, where jobs are scarce or of insecure tenure, where most men work on short-term projects such as building sites and road construction, there is a continually recurring need for the exchange of information about new jobs, and for a network of individuals who can be relied upon to help a man find his next job. For most men, it is kin who are most reliable as it is only kinsmen who can be trusted implicitly to act for one's best interests. "They wouldn't let none [jobs] go by if they thought it would suit you: they'd hear word of it and they'd let you know about it." The majority of the men can do better with their kinsmen's support than they could without it. Thus it is that in this atmosphere of chronic insecurity, the loyalties between kinsmen are an insurance policy and an avenue for advancement; and it is from these economic facts that much of the vitality of the masses' kinship ties in Aughnaboy stems. Those whose kinsmen are incapable of providing these services must turn for aid to "mates" or affines.

Few men like to be unemployed even though they are not in dire economic straits when out of work as they are free to draw the "brue" (unemployment benefits) which provides them with the basic necessities. If they are unemployed, they are denied the luxuries they may have become accustomed to; a single man living alone can draw only £1-10s-0d per week. In addition, they are denied the pride and satisfaction of being independent; and just as important, being unemployed is an admission that one's kin are insufficiently influential or reliable to find one a job. It is thus a blow to a man's self-esteem – and a threat to his kinsmen's prestige – to be unemployed for any length of time; and it is a matter for pride and boasting if one has never been on the "brue" in one's working life.

In Young and Willmott's (1957:95) words, family and kindred are a "kind of informal labour exchange" in which information and references for new jobs are readily and frequently exchanged. Men on the job are aware of both the positions which will be vacant and the kinsmen who may be in need of a job. When news of a job comes along, "you'd break the law if you told somebody who wasn't a relative." A man is expected to pressure his employer into hiring him. Trent got his nephew his first job in the following manner: "I just went up to the boss and told him that my brother's boy was the best, the very best, and would there be a position vacant that he could fill? The boss says yes, we'll try him out, and that's how I got Leonard the job."

Employers and a man's fellow employees are often forced to go along with this practice because it is generally agreed that a man "has right" to pressure his employer, and further, that a man also "has right" to succeed to a job previously held by a cognate – particularly by a patrinominal kinsman. Thus Charlie McTee wanted a berth on a more successful trawler, and when Charlie's father's brother retired from his berth on Henrik's trawler, Charlie "laid claim" to the job. Henrik felt that Charlie was a competent crewman, and so Charlie was hired. Of course, a man is by no means automatically entitled to succeed to a job, but if his skills and abilities are roughly equal to those of other candidates, then his claim is often honoured.

Kinsmen are also used to obtain higher-paying jobs. I have already described how fathers use their influence to obtain the best possible apprenticeships or first jobs for their sons. The jobs available to the majority of the villagers are ranked in salary terms. They range from County Council labourers such as street-sweepers at approximately £12 per week, to stone men who average £16 per week, to road labourers and unskilled construction workers who average approximately £20 per week (not including overtime), to skilled tradesmen and fishermen at £25–£30 per week. A man who has no trade is confined to fishing or unskilled labour on road or building construction; but within this category, he uses his kinsmen to find him the jobs with the highest hourly wage and the heaviest overtime, which together can raise his weekly income to £30 per week in peak periods. Among fishermen, the variation in income is primarily between vessels, for some skippers are more enterprising and successful than others; a man will use his network of kinsmen, as did Charlie McTee, to find him berths on the most successful vessels. Among skilled tradesmen, there are variations in the hourly wages paid by different employers and also in the amount of overtime likely to be available. The sixty- or seventy-hour-work week is most sought after, and it is among kinsmen that jobs of this value are most likely to be shared: "your friends are worth ten pound a week." Thus the individual exploits his kinsmen and they, in turn, exploit him.

There is a grading in the degree of "obligement" a man has to a specific kinsman, and the principles of kinship category and genealogical distance are the criteria which determine this degree for all class strata. The order of preference here, as elsewhere, is son, father, brother/brother's son/sister's son/father's brother's son/cognatic full cousin/patrinominal half cousin/ cognatic half cousin. If a man has one job to give, he will normally offer it to the kinsman closest to him, the evaluation of closeness being based on the formal kinship criteria, since helping a second cousin when a nephew needed a job would offend prevailing conceptions of decency and threaten the solidarity of his kin.

In a sample of 43 informants from all class strata, 20 obtained their present jobs through kinsmen, 17 through impersonal hiring, 4 through mates and neighbours, and 2 bought their own enterprises. Furthermore, at one time in their careers, 37 per cent of the men had obtained jobs for members of their families and kindred, and 95 percent had worked with family or kindred on the same job, either getting the job for the relatives or vice versa.

Since work is a matter for men, economic affairs primarily involve men and their patrinominal kin. It is patrinominal kin who are most likely to be appealed to for help and to be in a position to help: "say if your father was a mechanic, you'd be inclined to fall in line with him [as] they [patrinominal kin] could get you jobs better." In fact, the majority of jobs obtained through kinsmen were through family and patrinominal kin: of the 99 kinsmen with whom the 43 informants had worked, 53 were family (fathers, brothers, or sons), 23 were patrinominal kindred, 17 were affines, and only 6 were non-patrinominal cognatic kin.

Kinsmen are not only expected to help a man obtain a new and better job, they are also expected to help him keep it. They help him find a job with greater security of tenure, they are expected to cover up his mistakes on the job, and, if he is less than competent, to use what pressure they can to keep him employed. These expectations are rarely disappointed in Aughnaboy; one example is the way Smythe disguised his apprentice son's breaking of an expensive diamond saw in the stone yard; another involved McGregor who rushed his drunk uncle home and finished his quota for him, explaining his uncle's absence in terms of sickness; when Connell learned that a new order had been received for a large supply of the stone his own polishing operation was working on, he notified his cousin to switch to this order, for work on his operation would continue indefinitely while other orders were being rapidly filled and the men being laid off. However, absolute and unending loyalty is not expected. If a man falls so low in his work performance that he gains the contempt of his fellow workers, and especially if his own incompetence seriously compromises the income and efficiency of his kinsmen, then the ties that bind them may be broken.

Those who lack a network of family and kindred upon whom they can depend are seriously hampered in their search for jobs with decent wages, unless they develop a network of "workmates" over the years. It is almost impossible to obtain an apprenticeship in a good trade, and difficult to find well-paid jobs without a strong supportive network. The occupational history of an orphaned twenty-year-old who was raised by an unemployed and almost kinless uncle illustrates this relative insecurity. As a consequence of his kinlessness, Willy was restricted to the most menial and low-paying jobs, incapable of "getting a trade" or a decent wage. He left school at fifteen and got his first job at a home bakery through a half-cousin [who] "was working there, [and who] left the job and gave it to me." Willy soon grew tired of the working conditions and embarked on a series of jobs, the first of which was another low-paying job at an egg-packing factory. He left the factory after seven months and drove a van for a shopkeeper in Kildrum. "Then I went to the Donard Hotel shining silver – I just went down and got it, I knew there was plenty of work in the hotel in the summer time." In the autumn, he went to another hotel as a night porter. Still dissatisfied with the low pay, Willy found a mate and went to Leeds when he was seventeen, and "got a job driving a dumper for Wimpeys" until the job ended after four and one-half months. After this, he returned to Aughnaboy and found a job labouring on a bridge in Belfast – "I knew the ganger and went up to him and asked him for the job – I knew him well, he used to live beside us." Finally, Willy went to see his half-cousin who got him a slightly better paying job erecting scaffolds. "I've been with them for a year and a half now."

The kinless act as examples for the masses, underscoring the wisdom of delicately cultivating one's kin. The masses have an ideology in which all kin are bound by their common blood and common interest to help each other obtain and keep their jobs. To do so, their strategy involves creating a pool of information which is circulated exclusively among kin, and establishing ties of influence with their employers in order to maximize their chances of receiving new information and influencing recruiting. Men are continually being approached by their kin for work; and through this continuous activation of ties, a relationship of alliance and the exchange of favours is established and maintained. A man puts himself out to get his brother or cousin a job knowing that in due course he, himself, will call upon them to reciprocate. The refusal to help a kinsman in this manner is an infrequent event. A man suffers little in obtaining a job for his kinsman, provided they can be depended upon to do a "decent day's work" and not reflect badly on himself. The more favours he does, the more deeply he creates relations of debt and "obligement," and the less hesitation he will feel when he is forced to call upon them in turn. For the masses, economic wisdom is the root of kinship's moral imperatives.

THE ELITES: A BUREAUCRATIC IDEOLOGY AND STRATEGY

For the elites, class interests generate an ideology and strategy quite the opposite from those of the masses: the class interests of the masses dictate maximum dependence on kin, whereas the interests of the elites dictate a continual minimizing and blocking of obligations towards kin.

The elites' ideology regarding the employment of kin can be described as an *anti-kinship* or *bureaucratic* one: it emphasizes the values of administration by explicit rules and the separation of person from office, and minimizes the significance of kinship obligations in the occupational realm. The elites' economic interests necessitate a concentration on the efficiency and harmony of their enterprises, and the employment of their kin can only risk this efficiency. Consequently, elite ideology emphasizes the hazards of employing kin, and denigrates the significance of kinsmen in economic affairs. "Oh, relatives aren't so important nowadays." The elites emphasize the fact that resentments might be raised among non-kin employees if favouritism were shown towards kinsmen (favouritism that all know would be expected) – if, for example, incompetent kinsmen of the employer were kept on while competent men were denied work. In the words of one stone merchant, "I would tend to be against family connections in the business: if you were deciding who would be redundant, and you kept on the family, you would tend to get some grievances."

Further, employees expect their kin to give them special consideration which, if granted, could create resentment among non-kin employees, and if not granted, would infuriate kinsmen. Kinsmen expect special favours from those in a position to grant them; men expect their well-placed kin to preserve their jobs by not laying them off – "if there was a better job in the yard you'd try to get it off a relative – say a permanent job that doesn't slack off." They also expect their kin to help them get easier or higher-paying work – "if there was a soft job going, you'd look for it off a friend." Yet, other men on the job would resent continued favours to an employer's kinsmen if they themselves had served their employer for years without such favours, the employers say. Indeed, these conflicting pressures do place the employer in a difficult situation; they also provide him with the wherewithal for a legitimization of his unwillingness to hire kin; an unwillingness based on his commitment to a bureaucratic model emphasizing the efficiency of his enterprise.

It is said that the ambiguous authority relations with kin complicates phases of kinship relations. The elite holds that "you can't be a boss as easy with a friend as you can with an outsider; you can't yell at your uncle." It is thus held to be undesirable to hire kin, since it is awkward to give orders to a man who may be in a superior position in the kinship system, and difficult to discipline a person with whom one has shared many intimate and informal hours. The words of one shopkeeper express the fears that the elites have about exercising authority over kin on the job:

Say you hire your sister's boy. Well maybe one day you're not feeling good and he's late and you shout at him and he goes home and tells his mother and it goes through the whole family. But if he's no relation, well he'd take it as an admonition, and if he went home and told his mother, well she'd say 'you deserved it.' So all things considered, it's best not to work with relatives.

Essentially, the elites' bureaucratic model is that the efficiency and harmony of the enterprise is their primary concern and their ultimate responsibility. To ensure this efficiency and harmony, the elites must hire accordingly with complete disregard for favouring kin. Kinsmen, as a rule, offer only complications and obstacles to the efficiency of the enterprise.

To accomplish this, they use two different strategies simultaneously, the effect of which is to isolate them from their kin. Both foremen and friends are used as buffers between the elites and their importuning kin. Foremen are regularly used as buffers in the yards and on the construction sites. Here, if approached by kin asking for a job, the owners convey the impression that the yard foremen have full authority over all hiring; "I've no time for it myself." In this way, they relieve themselves of the responsibility of failing to hire kinsmen. Kinsmen are directed to the foremen who, acting upon the owners' instructions, do not hire him. If the transparency of this stratagem is apparent, the kinsmen, nevertheless, are forced to accept the reply, for to do otherwise would publicly challenge the honesty of the owners (kinsmen) and risk disrupting future relations. The foremen themselves are carefully selected by the owners, and not just for their occupational abilities; desirable foremen are those who are without kin, and indeed, most foremen are kinless.

While foremen act as buffers on the job, friends act as buffers in the social sphere. For most of the men of Aughnaboy, friends are "friends"; that is, kinsmen. But for the elites, social relations between non-kin – between friends – are formed to the exclusion of extra-familial kin. By extending their social lives into the realm of friendship, the elites limit the intrusion of kinsmen into their social and economic lives simply by spending their leisure hours in homes and country clubs which their kin cannot penetrate. MacAlinden, the stone merchant, has friends with whom he golfs, fishes, visits, and sails to the south of France. The dual strategies of having a kinless foreman and friends permit him to isolate himself from those who are continually asking favours – and with a minimum of discord.

Nevertheless, employers often find themselves in the position where they must hire one man in order to maintain the good will of one of their present employees who is kin to the applicant. A consequence of these pressures is that in any given enterprise there are likely to be men who have been recruited through a number of principles. In Horace Brady's stone yard which employs an average of sixteen men, none of his employees are his own kin, but some were hired on the basis of their kinship ties with other employees: "say we needed a young lad, well you'd ask the men in the yard if they had anybody near them needed a job." Some were hired on the basis of their known skills: "they were out of work and I knew they were good men, so I went to them and asked them would they be interested." Some heard about the jobs through mates or neighbours who were already employed in the yard and who vouched for their abilities, and some approached Horace directly and applied for the job: "they just came up to me and asked if there was anything going."

However, there are exceptions to the general rule of anti-kinship elites. I refer here to the elites in those occupations with special characteristics where kinsmen can be useful in the process of social mobility. These enterprises include fishing and some small businesses where a man can advance his kinsmen while bringing benefit to his own affairs. Fishing requires a high degree of trust in times of tension, and secrecy about past successes and future plans – qualities which are more likely to be found among kinsmen. Similarly, in small businesses where unusual amounts of labour are required in return for relatively low wages, such as the family tailor shop described below, kinsmen can be assets rather than liabilities. Further, on board a trawler or in a small business there are relatively few ranks and small differences in prestige in contrast to, say, a stone yard with its hierarchy, and therefore, a man is compromising neither his own prestige nor that of his kinsmen in hiring them.

But once an enterprise is established, the pressures of class interest which apply to the majority of the elites eventually reach the minority, and even individuals who move up from the masses to the elites in the course of their careers, such as trawler crewmen who purchase their own vessels, must inevitably adapt their ideology and strategies to their new position. An illustration of this transition is provided by the McLandress brothers whose affairs are discussed in detail throughout this monograph. Freddie was the skipper and owned half the trawler, while his brother Henry was a crewman and owned the other half. The other three in the crew consisted of a patrilateral first cousin of the two brothers, and two non-kin. During the early phases of their careers, the two brothers had pooled their labour and capital as crewmen and eventually saved enough to buy their own trawler. Once they had done so, Freddie's status as elder brother placed him as skipper, while Henry assumed a place as one of the crew, although deriving extra income from his share of the boat. Over the years, Henry began to drink heavily and his qualities as a crewman deteriorated: he consistently let the heavy work fall to the rest of the crew, dodged his duties, and even occasionally failed to turn up for a voyage. For ten years, Freddie endured the growing incompetence of his brother, but finally, he bought Henry's share of the vessel and removed him from the crew.

Increasingly subject to his commitment to the efficiency of the enterprise, the kinship model of economic obligations to kin became increasingly incongruent with Freddie's new class interests. To save the family's prestige in the community, he explained the action publicly not in terms of his own rejection of obligations towards kin, not in terms of a bureaucratic model, but by maintaining the public fiction that Henry was "sick" and could no longer be expected to work; privately, he admitted that his crew had "threatened to leave" *en masse* unless Henry were removed. Nonetheless, Freddie's future actions and statements of ideology were in accord with the elites' bureaucratic and 'anti-kinship' model of emphasizing the efficiency of the enterprise and minimizing obligations towards kin.

THE POOLING OF LABOUR AND CAPITAL

The pooling of labour and capital for common enterprises is the second major way in which kinsmen are utilized for economic purposes. Cross-culturally, this is by no means an uncommon situation, and Belshaw (1955), Epstein (1964), and many others have commented on the potential importance of kinship in this regard. As Firth (1964b) has observed, where social and moral bonds exist between kin, they can be readily adapted to the performance of significant collective operations. Kin groups can effectively mobilize labour and capital resources and "apply them to major capital investment." In Aughnaboy, the use of kin in such enterprises is a function of differential class interests and of the special character of certain industries, particularly farming, fishing, and small businesses.

The pooling of labour takes several forms. One is the simple exchange of economic services and favours among kinsmen, as when a plumber installs a new washer for his nephew, or a shopkeeper sells goods at a wholesale price to his brother. Another form is in fishing, where brothers or other close kin who are skippers distribute and minimize risk by fishing together. They search for fish together, keeping their vessels within, say, a radius of twenty miles, and when one man locates a large school of fish on his depth sounders, he notifies his kinsmen – preferably in a prearranged code indecipherable to other skippers. Such cooperation is occasionally attempted by non-kin, but is rarely effective or enduring, for men who are not kinsmen do not have implicit trust in each other. In these operations, trust is essential, for if the school of fish disappears by the time the other skipper arrives, suspicion and distrust may result and soon disrupt the cooperative effort.

Farmers too, often pool their labour among kin in the institution known as "working mean," as hired hands are expensive, unreliable, and hard to find. When labour requirements are the highest in the agricultural cycle, such as in the harvesting and threshing periods, brothers or cousins will work each other's fields in turn, sharing the work load between two or three farms. These cooperative farming groups, however, do not require high levels of trust, for the work is clear-cut and carried out in front of everyone in the fields. Consequently, neighbours are often incorporated in these shared labour teams, but kinsmen, more than neighbours, can be relied upon to leave their own farms when a kinsman needs help, to do more than their share of work. Thus, these shared labour teams are normally kin-based.

In some businesses too, the pooling of labour can be significant, particularly when men must work long hours for uncertain returns in the early stages of a business. This is illustrated in the case of George McGregor. George's father's father James and James's brother were both apprenticed to "the tailoring" in the 1840s; in 1847, James set up a shop in Aughnaboy, and his brother set up another shop in another county. James married and, in turn, taught his two sons the tailoring business; William and Hugh accordingly joined their father in the shop. William did not marry and died childless, and so the shop and tailoring business gradually came under the control of Hugh's sons, including George. George worked all his life with his six brothers, his father, and uncle in their tailoring establishment. "I was never fond of the tailoring and would rather have gone to sea, but there was plenty of work in our shop and my health wasn't the best, so I forgot about sailoring and went into the shop and learned the tailoring from my father and my uncle."

By the time George and his brothers approached retirement age in the late 1940s, the local manufacture of clothing was being out-priced by the national brand-name manufacturers, and the demand was steadily falling for McGregor's products. When they retired shortly after, local manufacture of clothing ceased, and instead, the next generation – George's brother's two sons – set up a retail draper's shop, selling manufactured clothing to the villagers. They began their new business by working without pay in the evenings with their wives tending shop without pay in the day. With this system, all the early profits of the enterprise could be ploughed back into the business and heavy debts could be avoided – something that would be impossible with non-kin who would expect to be paid from the beginning. The enterprise continued as long as economic conditions allowed. When conditions changed and new opportunities became available, some of the next generation went into other occupations – two are school teachers – while others changed the nature of their business to suit the new market.

Another major use of kinship ties is the pooling of capital for the formation of kin-based enterprises. This is occasionally found in small businesses: George McGregor's two nephews pooled their capital as well as their labour to buy the initial stock of draper's goods necessary for setting up their shop. But it is most common in fishing which provides ready avenues for large-scale investment, and which is highly favourable to kin-based enterprises. The case of the McLandress brothers is a useful example. The brothers purchased their first trawler in the following manner: four of them, all crewmen on various skippers' vessels, pooled their savings after the war when new government subsidies were made available to individuals with relatively small amounts of capital. These subsidies provided an outright grant of 33 percent of the cost of a new trawler, and a low-interest loan for 52 percent of the cost price; for a second-hand trawler, a low-interest loan without the grant was provided for 85 percent of the cost of the trawler. Thus, it was possible to buy a new and well-equipped trawler for an initial outlay of approximately £4,500, or a good used trawler for as little as £1,500. By pooling their savings, the four brothers managed to raise the payment required for a new trawler. Each brother then owned one share of the vessel; the eldest and most aggressive brother acted as skipper, and one younger brother and one patrilateral parallel cousin were taken on as crew. Fishing regularly, they used the bulk of their profits to pay off the loan on the trawler, and to amass capital for the initial payment on a second boat. This second vessel was purchased a few years later, and the process was repeated yet again in 1960 to buy a third trawler. Good fishing in the years immediately after the war, high fish prices, the increased technical efficiency and reliability of the post-war diesel trawlers, and the ready availability of government grants and subsidies made possible the large-scale formation of capital through the pooling of labour and capital in kin-based enterprises.

This pooling of labour and capital is most significant in occupations such as fishing and small businesses which require high levels of cooperation, good faith and secrecy while providing avenues for social mobility, yet which are not subject to the administrative rules forbidding nepotism in hiring, or requiring high levels of specialized skills that characterize the national and multi-national corporations. Although the actual large-scale pooling of labour and capital for common enterprises is practised by only a minority of the elites, the existence of this kin-based mechanism provides an important avenue for material and social advancement as well as the most efficient and economic way to run certain operations.

CREDIT

Family and kindred are also important economically as sources of credit, and in this regard there is no dissensus. Kin are the final buttress against catastrophe for all the social strata; for the obligations towards kin are the strongest, and the mutual interest of kin in husbanding their prestige makes it incumbent on them to help one another on such occasions. When Reggie Andrews drank himself out of his business, it was his two brothers who hired the lawyers to go through the bankruptcy proceedings, who paid off Reggie's debts, and used their capital to try to establish him in another business. Even though they publicly explained their actions in terms of the kinship system's profound moral obligations towards brothers (with private reference to the malicious talk which would ensue if they failed to help), it is apparent that if they had not made these considerable sacrifices, their own prestige would have been seriously reduced and their reputations degraded.

CONCLUSION

To conclude this chapter, I have tried to describe the economic nature of much of kinship behaviour, and to do so with reference to the variation in such behaviour which is generated by different class interests. For all men, kin are vitally important as sources of credit in catastrophe. For men in certain industries whose special characteristics require high levels of cooperation and secrecy, kin are important for the pooling of labour and capital. But it is with regard to hiring and occupation that dissensus is apparent, that class interests dictate whether or not it is to the advantage of an individual to honour his obligations (or indeed, even to recognize them) towards his kinsmen; and it is here that separate and conflicting ideologies and their associated strategies parallel the opposing interests of the class strata. In the concluding chapter, I shall try to sketch the parameters and the origins of these distinct ideologies.

Summary and Conclusions

9

When I began the work which culminated in this volume, I saw my task as a simple one: to describe *the* kinship ideology of Aughnaboy, and to relate the ideology to the actual patterns of behaviour in the conventional structuralist manner. At this level, my findings have not been very different from those reported for many other parts of "peasant" Europe: among Campbell's Sarakatsani shepherds, the family is "the centre of the shepherd's world." Within the family, the individual "finds support, affection, and a sense of moral obligation," and these attitudes are extended by association to cognatic kin (1964:38). In rural South Wales (Loudon, 1961), the sense of identity and obligation derived from kinship relations is associated with kin groups with three primary functions: kin are extensively mobilized for ceremonial occasions such as weddings and funerals; they provide an important resource for identifying and evaluating behaviour; and they can be mobilized quickly to support individuals in times of social or economic crisis.

Yet, it soon became apparent that in Aughnaboy there was no single "master system," no integrated "common whole" of shared customs and values (cf. Arensberg and Kimball, 1968:310 ff.). The village's kinship system could be explained neither in terms of unity, nor of integration. Kinship had to be related to other institutional sets because there were different systems, each an adaptation to a particular set of economic constraints. Contradictory and mutually exclusive ideologies jostled in the marketplace.

These varying ideologies are derived primarily from the influence of social class upon Aughnaboy's kinship system. Given the absence of comparative data, it is essentially a matter for speculation whether this intense interaction between class and kinship is a phenomenon peculiar to Aughnaboy. It may be that Aughnaboy's characteristics as a traditional peasant community in the process of adapting to an industrial economy create a situation which is peculiarly conducive to class analysis. However, a more likely explanation is that the neglect of class is a consequence of the kinds of social units ethnographers have customarily studied. In Europe, much research has been done with either relatively simple and undifferentiated villages, or with single-class urban samples. As examples of the former, I cite Campbell (1964) and Stirling (1965), and as examples of the latter, Firth's (1956) study of working class Londoners, and Bell's

(1968) study of middle class Swansea. In this respect, Aughnaboy has proven a singularly useful example, for despite its being one small village, it nevertheless provides a wide range of social and economic differentiation.

A. Class and Kinship: Three Ideologies

The nature of Perrin economic and social reality is such that individuals are presented with quite different opportunities. Further, their differential position in the economic hierarchy presents them with varying expectations and interests. Consequently, the villagers have evolved three alternative ideologies as an adaptation to this reality and as a means of both explaining and justifying their actions. These ideologies are not necessarily fixed for the life of an individual, for a man may rise or fall in the economic hierarchy, and be forced to modify his position accordingly. But the majority of the villagers spend their adult lives embracing one ideology and pursuing its appropriate strategies. For all men, the family is the ultimate unit of obligation. But beyond the family, individuals choose cognates, *or* affines, *or* friends, as their boundary to the dominion of obligation.

1. A kinship ideology: cognates. For the majority of the population of Aughnaboy, for the various strata I have designated as the masses, obligation and exchange are expressed in terms of a cognatic kinship ideology. Rights and duties are distributed among a wide range of cognates up to, and occasionally including, third cousins. Although the degree of obligation is finely graded according to kinship category and genealogical distance, the entire ego-focused group is potentially on call for any aid required. The solidarity of cognatic kin is graphically expressed in the local phrase, "If you kick one of them, the rest of them limp."

An almost mystical bond – made more intense and socially ratified by its ancient roots – is seen to link those of common descent. The belief that they "share the one blood" creates a bond of loyalty, trust, and cooperation which they see as an impossibility between two unrelated men. Assisting kin whenever called upon and, in the case of very close kin, even before called upon is the generalized obligation which ties kinsmen to one another. This ideology is summarized in the following remarks by informants:

You're more or less a *part* of a relation. A neighbour? You're just a neighbour because you live beside them. You'd put more confidence, more trust in them (kin). Anybody can be your neighbours. When it comes to the pinch, you might help a neighbour, but you wouldn't feel the duty that you would with a relative.

More or less you would expect relatives to help. You would feel more a sense of duty to them than you would to outsiders – they've got their own relatives. And you'd get your own people in first in whatever jobs there was going.

For the majority of the masses, notions of "the one blood" provide the rationale for the extension of obligation to a wide range of cognatic kin; and the boundaries between familial and extra-familial kin are blurred appropriately. This is not an arbitrary custom; rather, it is a rational adaptation by individuals who occupy a vulnerable position in the economic hierarchy. By distributing obligation, they distribute risk; the network of cognates functions as both an insurance policy and a potential channel for social mobility.

2. An anti-kinship ideology: friendship. For the elites, however, extra-familial kin are only an encumbrance, a potential obstacle to the efficiency of their enterprises. For them, friendship replaces kinship as the ideology of obligation and trust. For the class-generated interests of the elites dictate a continual minimizing and blocking of obligations to extra-familial kin. On the other hand, friendship may begin as a strategy for the resolution of the conflict between the expectations of kin and the demands for efficiency of the enterprise, but it becomes an alternative ideology – with its own sentiment and emotional charge – to the primacy of the cognatic group.

Although it is primarily an elite adaptation, this anti-kinship or friendship ideology also replaces the quasi-mystical doctrine of "one blood" for those of the masses who through death, emigration, or dispute, are kinless. The behavioural correlate of this ideological shift is the transfer of loyalty and aid to non-kin friends. Remarks of informants illustrate this alternative ideology.

I'd go to a mate first if I was in trouble. I suppose it's a matter of losing face among your family. A mate would keep his mouth shut, but your family, it'd (your trouble) be through the whole family and then it'd spread through the whole community. If the breadwinner lets the side down, he doesn't want it spread about.

If you were in trouble, it's not your relatives, it's the outsider that would help you. Your relatives would do nothing for you. You could rely more on your neighbours than on your relatives. Your relatives, they would throw it up to you if they ever did anything for you – that's never that way with an outsider.

For the elites, then (and for the small proportion of the masses who are rendered kinless), their position in the economic hierarchy with its attendant interests and obligations dictates an ideology which denies the significance of extra-familial kin and creates a culturally justified explanation for alternative modes of association.

3. An affinal ideology. There is a third ideology in Aughnaboy; I refer here to the affinal ideology which repudiates both the cognatic and friendship constructions. The occurrence of this model is infrequent and is confined to the few propertyless men who have married women with property, or to those kinless men who have married women whose cognates have influence in their (the men's) occupations. The nature of their participation in the social and economic system and their need for justifying their actions dictate an ideology which assigns primacy to affines. Angus, from County Tyrone, works in his wife's shop:

When a man or a woman are married, it's the wife's people that come first. The husband's people are put in the background. The wife says we're going to my mother and he just tags along. She's not really interested in his people. If he says come to ours (his kin), she says she's got something to do.

John, an only child, works with his in-laws:

In-laws are relations in a way. You find yourself gradually being looked on in that way. If you married in, you're all right. They wouldn't put you out of a job to put one of their own in, because that would reflect back on your wife. I was a fisherman for a while, and my father-in-law was down in the yard (stone), and he got me the job there. I been there ever since. If anything goes wrong at the work, you go to your relations and it's an unwritten law that you don't say anything. In the yard, there'd be the wife's relations and they'd talk to me.

This affinal ideology is a rare one in Aughnaboy, for it is an admission of a man's low prestige to depend upon his in-laws, and an admission of the inferiority of his family for him to depend upon the social or economic capital of his wife. But for those whose socio-economic status is of this kind, an ideology evolves in which both cognatic and friendship models are supplanted by an affinal ideology which assigns obligation and trust (and even a measure of sentiment) to the spouse's cognates.

In sum then, there are three contradictory ideologies and associated behaviour patterns which co-exist in Aughnaboy: a friendship ideology held primarily by the elites, a cognatic ideology held primarily by the masses, and an affinal ideology which is found primarily among those men who are dependent upon their wives' property. The ideology which an individual will follow and the behaviour which he will adopt are shaped and patterned by his position in the economic hierarchy.

B. The Primacy of Economics

In this essay, I have tried to test the applicability of the notions elaborated by Worsley and Leach for the analysis of behaviour between kinsmen in one Irish village. It has been clear that in this heterogeneous and stratified village with one foot in its peasant past and the other in a modern capitalist economy, individuals are provided with alternative adaptive strategies. The choice of their strategies, however, is not a random act. Choice is clearly patterned – in terms of the individual's varying position in the socio-economic hierarchy.

Class membership invests individuals with expectations and interests which are, at times, in accord with those in other classes and, at times, in conflict. When they coincide, then kinship ideology and behaviour can be described in terms of a *consensus omnium*, as in the system of kin classification and categories which is shared throughout the village. When, however, the interests of the different classes place them clearly in conflict, then members of the different classes opt for alternative ideologies and strategies. The masses operate primarily in terms of a "traditional" kinship ideology; the elites have evolved their own adaptation of an anti-kinship model. Thus it is that whereas all class strata classify kin in the same manner and regard the family as the paramount unit, there are major differences in their behaviour *vis-à-vis* extra-familial kin. Thus it is that the elite strata minimize obligations within the kindred and have developed strategies for blocking social and economic interaction with cognates, whereas the masses strata maximize their obligations towards their kinsmen and continually reaffirm these obligations through intense social interaction and the continuing exchange of economic favours.

The quasi-mysticism in Aughnaboy's kinship ideology – of the name, the blood, and the home place – must be seen here in its true light as cultural justifications for hard economic facts, as consequence and not cause. I do not wish to suggest for a moment that the villagers are cynical manipulators of a system. They are not. The kinship system and other traditional values have powerful emotional gratifications for them. But kinship values are impossible to sustain in the face of strong economic pressure. As among the Tallensi, "the sentiment of solidarity soon dissolves when material interests clash" (Worsley, 1956). As for the Nupe, kinship relations for the higher strata have been overwhelmed by the "impersonal relations of the market" (Nadel, 1942:376). The inhabitants of Aughnaboy are "decent" and "kindly" people who love their kinsmen. But in the course of their adaptation to their difficult economy, it is their position *vis-à-vis* the means of production which ultimately patterns their social lives. Aughnaboy's kinship system has been profoundly influenced by the changing economic conditions. Wage labour and social mobility have operated together to undermine the traditional kinship structure. Ultimately, the explanation for differential behaviour lies in the nature of the economic system.

References

ARENSBERG, CONRAD
1937 *The Irish Countryman*. Cambridge, Macmillan.
ARENSBERG, CONRAD and SOLON T. KIMBALL
1940 *Family and Community in Ireland*. (2nd Ed., 1968). Cambridge, Harvard University Press.
BAILEY, F. G.
1971 *Gifts and Poison*. Toronto, Copp Clark.
BAX, MART
1970 "Patronage Irish Style: Irish Politicians as Brokers." *Sociollogische Gids*, 17:179–191.
BAX, MART
1971 "Kiesstelsel en Leider – Volgelingrelaties in Ierland." *Mens en Maatschappij*, 4:366–75.
BAX, MART
1973 "Harpstrings and Confessions." University of Amsterdam, Unpublished Ms.
BELL, COLIN
1968 *Middle Class Families*. London, Routledge and Kegan Paul.
BELSHAW, C. S.
1955 "In Search of Wealth." *American Anthropological Association*, Memoir No. 80.
BOTT, ELIZABETH
1957 *Family and Social Network*. (2nd Ed., 1971). London, Tavistock.
BUCHANAN, R. H.
1958 "Rural Change in an Irish Townland." *Advancement of Science*, 56:291–300.
CAMPBELL, J. K.
1964 *Honour, Family and Patronage*. Oxford, Clarendon Press.
CONNELL, K. H.
1962 "Peasant Marriage in Ireland: Its Structure and Development Since the Famine." *Economic History Review*, 2nd Series, 14:502–23.
CONNELL, K. H.
1968 "Catholicism and Marriage in the Century after the Famine." In K. H. Connell (ed.), *Irish Peasant Society*. Oxford, Oxford University Press.

CRESSWELL, ROBERT
1969 *Une Communauté Rurale de L'Irlande.* Paris, Institut D'Ethnologie Musee de L'Homme.

DAHRENDORF, RALF
1959 *Class and Class Conflict in Industrial Society.* Stanford, Stanford University Press.

DUNNING, R. W.
1960 "Differentiation of Status in Subsistence Level Societies." *Transactions of the Royal Society of Canada*, 54:25–32.

EPSTEIN, SCARLETT
1964 "Personal Capital Formation among the Tolai of New Britain." In R. Firth and B. S. Yamey (eds.), *Capital, Saving and Credit in Peasant Societies.* London, George Allen and Unwin.

EVANS, ESTYN
1967 *Mourne Country.* Dundalk, Dundalgan Press.

FARBER, BERNARD
1971 *Kinship and Class.* New York, Basic Books.

FIRTH, RAYMOND
1946 *Malay Fishermen.* London, Routledge and Kegan Paul.

FIRTH, RAYMOND
1956 *Two Studies of Kinship in London.* London School of Economics Monographs on Social Anthropology, No. 15. London, Athlone Press.

FIRTH, RAYMOND
1964a "Family and Kinship in Industrial Society." In Paul Halmos (ed.), *The Development of Industrial Societies.* Keele, Sociological Review Monograph.

FIRTH, RAYMOND
1964b "Capital, Saving and Credit in Peasant Societies: a Viewpoint from Economic Anthropology." In Raymond Firth and B. S. Yamey (eds.), *Capital, Saving and Credit in Peasant Societies.* London, George Allen and Unwin.

FIRTH, RAYMOND, JANE HUBERT and ANTHONY FORGE
1969 *Families and Their Relatives.* London, Routledge and Kegan Paul.

FORTES, M.
1949 *The Web of Kinship among the Tallensi.* London, Oxford University Press.

FORTES, M.
1962 "Introduction." In Jack Goody (ed.), *The Developmental Cycle in Domestic Groups.* Cambridge Papers in Social Anthropology, No. 1. Cambridge, Cambridge University Press.

FOX, J. R.
1963 "Structure of Personal Names on Tory Island." *Man*, 63:153–55.

Fox, J. R.
1965 "The Structure of Marriage on Tory Island." Unpublished Ms.
Fox, J. R.
1966 "Kinship and Land Tenure on Tory Island." *Ulster Folklife*, 12:1–17.
Fox, J. R.
1967 "Tory Island." In B. Benedict (ed.), *Problems of Smaller Territories*. London, Athlone Press.
Fox, J. R.
1968 "Multilingualism in Two Communities." *Man* (N.S.), 3:456–64.
Freeman, J. D.
1961 "On the Concept of the Kindred." *Journal of the Royal Anthropological Institute*, 91:192–220.
Government Publications
1841–1861 *Census of Ireland*. Dublin and Belfast.
1846 *The Parliamentary-Gazetteer of Ireland*. Dublin, Government of Ireland.
1949 *Marriage (Prohibited Degrees of Relationship) Act (Northern Ireland)*. Belfast.
1960 *Inheritance (Family Provision) Act (Northern Ireland)*. Belfast.
Gulliver, P. H.
1971 *Neighbours and Networks*. Berkeley, University of California Press.
Harris, Rosemary
1961 "The Selection of Leaders in Ballybeg, Northern Ireland." *The Sociological Review*, 9:137–49.
Harris, Rosemary
1972 *Prejudice and Tolerance in Ulster*. Manchester, Manchester University Press.
Hollingshead, A. B.
1950 "Class Differences in Family Stability." *The Annals of the American Academy of Political and Social Science*, 39–46.
Humphreys, A. J.
1966 *New Dubliners*. London, Routledge and Kegan Paul.
Kane, Eileen
1968 "Man and Kin in Donegal: A Study of Kinship Functions in a Rural Irish and an Irish-American Community." *Ethnology*, 7:245–58.
Leach, Edmund
1961 *Pul Eliya: a Village in Ceylon*. Cambridge, Cambridge University Press.
Leyton, Elliott
1966 "Conscious Models and Dispute Regulation in an Ulster Village." *Man* (N.S.), 1:534–42.

LEYTON, ELLIOTT
  1970a "Spheres of Inheritance in Aughnaboy." *American Anthropologist*, 72:1378–88.
LEYTON, ELLIOTT
  1970b "Death and Authority in the Fishing Industry." *Resurgence*, 3:12–13.
LEYTON, ELLIOTT
  1974 "Opposition and Integration in Ulster." *Man* (N.S.), 9:185–98.
LEYTON, ELLIOTT
  1975 "Irish Friends and 'Friends': the Nexus of Friendship, Kinship and Class in Aughnaboy." In Elliott Leyton (ed.), *The Compact: Selected Dimensions of Friendship*. St. John's, Institute of Social & Economic Research, Memorial University of Newfoundland.
LINTON, RALPH
  1959 "The Natural History of the Family." In R. N. Anshen (ed.), *The Family, Its Function and Destiny*. New York, Harper.
LOUDON, JOE
  1961 "Kinship and Crisis in South Wales." *British Journal of Sociology*, 12:333–50.
MESSENGER, J. C.
  1968 "Types and Causes of Disputes in an Irish Community." *Eire-Ireland*, 3:27–37.
MESSENGER, J. C.
  1969 *Inis Beag: Isle of Ireland*. New York, Holt, Rinehart and Winston.
NADEL, S. F.
  1942 *A Black Byzantium*. London, Oxford University Press.
PARSONS, TALCOTT
  1954 "The Present Position and Prospects of Systematic Theory in Sociology." In Talcott Parsons (ed.), *Essays in Sociological Theory*. Glencoe, Free Press.
PITT-RIVERS, JULIAN
  1960 "Social Class in a French Village." *Anthropological Quarterly*, 33:1–13.
RADCLIFFE-BROWN, A. R.
  1950 "Introduction." In A. R. Radcliffe-Brown and Daryll Forde (eds.), *African Systems of Kinship and Marriage*. London, Oxford University Press.
RADCLIFFE-BROWN, A. R.
  1952 *Structure and Function in Primitive Society*. London, Cohen and West.
RUNCIMANN, W. G.
  1969 "The Three Dimensions of Social Inequality." In André Beteille (ed.), *Social Inequality*. London, Penguin Books.

STENNING, D. J.
   1962 "Household Viability among the Pastoral Fulani." In Jack Goody
   (ed.), *The Developmental Cycle in Domestic Groups*. Cambridge Papers in Social Anthropology, No. 1. Cambridge, Cambridge University Press.
STIRLING, PAUL
   1965 *Turkish Village*. London, Weidenfeld and Nicolson.
STREIB, GORDON F.
   1973 "Social Stratification in the Republic of Ireland: the Horizontal and
   the Vertical Mosaic. *Ethnology*, 12:341–57.
SYMES, D. G.
   1972 "Farm Household and Farm Performance: a Study of Twentieth
   Century Changes in Ballyferriter, Southwest Ireland." *Ethnology*,
   11:25–38.
WORSLEY, P. M.
   1956 "The Kinship System of the Tallensi: a Revaluation." *Journal of
   the Royal Anthropological Institute*, 86:37–75.
YOUNG, MICHAEL and PETER WILLMOTT
   1957 *Family and Kinship in East London*. London, Routledge and Kegan
   Paul.

List of Institute Publications

Studies

1 TOM PHILBROOK. *Fisherman, Logger, Merchant, Miner: Social Change and Industrialism in Three Newfoundland Communities*

2 JOHN SZWED. *Private Cultures and Public Imagery: Interpersonal Relations in a Newfoundland Peasant Society*

3 JIM FARIS. *Cat Harbour: A Newfoundland Fishing Settlement*

4 SHMUEL BEN-DOR. *Makkovik: Eskimos and Settlers in a Labrador Community*

5 MELVIN M. FIRESTONE. *Brothers and Rivals: Patrilocality in Savage Cove*

6 NOEL IVERSON and D. RALPH MATTHEWS. *Communities in Decline: An Examination of Household Resettlement in Newfoundland*

7 CATO WADEL. *Marginal Adaptations and Modernization in Newfoundland: A Study of Strategies and Implications of Resettlement and Redevelopment of Outport Fishing Communities*

8 ROBERT L. DEWITT. *Public Policy and Community Protest: The Fogo Case*

9 OTTAR BROX. *Newfoundland Fishermen in the Age of Industry. A Sociology of Economic Dualism*

10 LOUIS J. CHIARAMONTE. *Craftsman-Client Contracts: Interpersonal Relations in a Newfoundland Fishing Community*

11 CATO WADEL. *Now, Whose Fault is That? The Struggle for Self-Esteem in the Face of Chronic Unemployment*

12 GEORG HENRIKSEN. *Hunters in the Barrens: The Naskapi on the Edge of the White Man's World*

13 ROBERT MCGHEE. *Beluga Hunters: An Archaeological Reconstruction of the History and Culture of the Mackenzie Delta Kittegaryumiut*

14 ANTHONY P. COHEN. *The Management of Myths: The Politics of Legitimation in a Newfoundland Community*

15 ELLIOTT LEYTON. *The One Blood: Kinship and Class in an Irish Village*

Papers

1 MICHAEL L. SKOLNIK (ed.). *Viewpoints on Communities in Crisis*

2 ROBERT PAINE (ed.). *Patrons and Brokers in the East Arctic*

3 ELLIOTT LEYTON (ed.). *The Compact: Selected Dimensions of Friendship*

4 M. M. R. FREEMAN (ed.). *Intermediate Adaptation in Newfoundland and the Arctic: A Strategy of Social and Economic Development*

5 RAOUL ANDERSEN and CATO WADEL (eds.). *North Atlantic Fishermen: Anthropological Essays on Modern Fishing*